W9-AAD-889

THE WATTS HISTORY OF SPORTS

basketball

A History of Hoops

MARK STEWART

FRANKLIN WATTS
A Division of Grolier Publishing
New York • London • Hong Kong • Sydney
Danbury, Connecticut

Cover design by Dave Klaboe   Series design by Molly Heron
Photographs ©: Allsport USA: 78 (Rich Clarkson), 106, cover top center (Scott Cunningham), 105, cover bottom far left, (Mike Powell); Andrew D. Bernstein: 123; AP/Wide World Photos: cover center far right, cover bottom right, 21, 35, 38, 44, 51, 57, 69, 83, 93, 95, 97, 98, 99, 112, 113, 117; Archive Photos: 54 (APA), 42 (Sporting News), 7; Corbis-Bettman: 126, 129, cover bottom far left (Agence France Presse), cover top left (Kevin J. Larkin), Dick Raphael: cover top right, 89; Heinz Kluetmeier: 74; NBA Photos: 119 (Bill Baptist), 124 (Andrew D. Bernstein), 107 (Nathaniel S. Butler), 103 (Jim Cummins), 127 (Fernando Medina), 66, 91 (Ken Regan), 87 (Wen Roberts), 96 (Al Satterwhite) cover bottom left, 85; Sportschrome, Inc.: 111 (Brian Drake), 114; Team Stewart, Inc.: 26, 30 , 31, 33 (Basketball Hall of Fame),15 (Converse 1961 Basketball Yearbook), 68 (Dell Sports Magazine Basketball), 22 (Naismith Memorial Basketball Hall of Fame), 56 (Official Collegiate Basketball Record Book), 40 (Olimpia 1936), 17, 25 (Sport Kings Chewing Gum, Boston), 50, 58 (Sport Magazine), 45 (Sports Review Magazine), 90 (Topps Chewing Gum, Inc.), 60 (Tribute to Mr. Basketball), 43 (WMGM Sport Calendar), 118 (YWCA); Time Inc. Picture Collection: 72 (Tony Triolo); UPI/Corbis-Bettmann: cover center right, cover center left, cover center far left, 5 ,24, 36, 62, 70, 71, 75, 81, 82, 86, 88, 94, 102, 108,109.

Visit Franklin Watts on the Internet at:
http://publishing.grolier.com

Stewart, Mark
Basketball: a history of hoops / Mark Stewart.
p. cm. — (The Watts history of sports)
Includes bibliographical references and index.
Summary: Discusses the origins and evolution of the sport of basketball, as well as important events and key personalities in both college and professional versions of the game.
ISBN 0-531-11492-9
1. Basketball—United States—History—Juvenile literature.
[1. Basketball—History.] I. Title II. Series.
GV883.S784 1998
796.323 ' 0973—dc21 98-25040
CIP
AC

Library of Congress Cataloging-in-Publication Data

Printed in the United States of America
3 4 5 6 7 8 9 10 R 07 06 05 04

CONTENTS

THE HISTORY OF BASKETBALL

"Naismith-Ball" Is Born

Healthy mind, healthy body. During the 1880s, followers of a man named Dudley Sargent believed that these two qualities were inseparable. Sargent was the 19th century's version of a fitness guru, and his views on the benefits of exercise won him great acclaim. As the first professor of physical training at Harvard University, he was the recognized authority on subjects ranging from gymnastics to personal hygiene. Many of the day's leading educators, politicians, and businessmen sought his advice on how to make Americans healthier, while many of Sargent's students at Harvard went on to become future leaders.

One of Sargent's young disciples was Luther Gulick, a New York University medical student who earned extra money as a superintendent at a gymnasium operated by the Young Men's Christian Association (YMCA). After graduating in 1887, Gulick moved to Springfield, Massachusetts, and became involved with the YMCA. By 1891, he was one of the organization's most active and influential members. As the head of physical education at the YMCA's School for Christian Workers, he was responsible for the fitness of the student body. In the fall, football was the activity of choice; in the spring, baseball kept the young men occupied. But during the long, dreary Massachusetts winters, there was nothing in the way of team sports to engage the competitive spirit. Group exercise was limited to calisthenics and marching drills, the monotony of which was sometimes broken up by equally dull activities such as tumbling, throwing a medicine ball, or working with weights and pulleys. Not surprisingly, the students—most of whom were in their twenties—dreaded the hour they were compelled to spend in the gymnasium each day.

One group of 18 students, who were being trained together as future YMCA general secretaries, was particularly reluctant to hit the gym. So stubborn in their resistance were they that Dr. Gulick felt it necessary to come up with a new activity that would actually make them look forward to indoor exercise. Dr. Gulick asked two of his instructors to devise a game that would be athletically challenging, yet include aspects of sports with which the students were

Dr. James Naismith, the father of basketball.

already familiar. What these men came up with apparently failed to meet Gulick's lofty expectations, for he then turned to a 30-year-old faculty member named Dr. James Naismith, who had once mentioned at a faculty meeting that the problem was not with the men but with the activities. As far as Dr. Gulick was concerned, this incorrigible bunch was now Naismith's responsibility.

Naismith possessed a degree in theology and was a graduate of McGill University in Montreal, Canada. At McGill, Naismith had starred on the soccer, rugby, and track teams, and was twice honored as the school's top all-around athlete. Naismith, then, had plenty of experience with sports, which would help him deal with the task at hand: Not only would he have to devise a game interesting enough for vigorous young men, he would also have to judge where to set appropriate limits in terms of skill, physical contact, and endurance.

At first Naismith tried to create indoor versions of such sports as lacrosse and rugby, but they proved too rough. With just one day left before he had to report to Dr. Gulick, he had gotten absolutely nowhere. Determined not to give up, Naismith sat down and made a systematic analysis of all popular sports. He decided that his new sport would have to use a ball—definitely a large one, because a small ball almost always required some kind of equipment. From rugby and football he borrowed the lateral, or "pass."

As for how points would be scored, Naismith wanted to avoid ground-level goals because that would mean players would be throwing the ball as hard as they could. This was not a good idea for a game played among 18 men in a confined space. He thought back to a childhood game called Duck on a Rock, in which the winner knocked an object off a rock by hitting it with a small stone. A large "guard rock" was placed in front of the object, requiring a player to gently arc his stone over this barrier in order to win. Thus Naismith decided his game should have an elevated goal. This would require the player throwing the ball to use finesse instead of raw power, and it also would prevent defensive players from massing in front of the goal to stop him.

The following morning Naismith asked Pop Stebbins, the school janitor, for a couple of boxes that he might use as goals. Pop replied that he had no boxes, but there were a couple of old peach baskets in the cellar. That was fine, the doctor said. Naismith climbed a ladder with hammer and nails, and affixed the peach baskets to the rail at opposite ends of the gymnasium's balcony. As it so happened, the top rim of the basket was 10 feet off the gymnasium floor. Then he nailed up a set of rules for his 18 students to read. When the class filed in at noon, Naismith promised them that if they did not like this game, that would be the end of the great experiment. He divided the men into teams of nine, positioned the two tallest players in between the baskets, and tossed a soccer ball in the air for them to battle over.

That first game of basketball was a little different than the game that would take shape over the next half-century. Players were not allowed to move once they received a pass, and no one had even thought of dribbling the ball. A foul was called for any infraction, not just physical contact, and a player committing a second foul was remanded to a penalty area. Throwing the ball in the basket was practically impossible; there was no other sport at the time which required the technique of "shooting a ball"

The gymnasium at the YMCA's School for Christian Workers in Springfield, Massachusetts, where basketball was born in 1891.

so no one was quite sure how to do it. The nine players were divided as follows: three defenders, or "guards," stayed near their own basket; three men stationed themselves in the middle of the court as "centers"; and three shooters whom Naismith called "wings." Some remember the final score as 1-0, while others recall that a number of goals were made—no one bothered to chronicle the details of that first game until many years had passed. Nevertheless, this was how basketball was born. Unlike almost every other team sport of the time, it did not evolve from some other game or pastime. It quite literally sprang from the imagination of one human being.

Like the score, the actual date of the first game is also something of a mystery. What is known, however, is that the entire school soon found about Naismith's new game and students would rush over to the gym each day at noon to watch it being played. Several students showed the game to friends and family over Christmas break, which suggests that Naismith first introduced basketball to his class some time in December of 1891. In January, a returning student by the name of Frank Mahan suggested this new sport be called "Naismith-Ball." Naismith appreciated the gesture, but replied that a name like that would surely kill the game. Mahan agreed, and suggested another name: Basketball.

In the January 15, 1892 edition of the *Triangle* (a newspaper sent to all of the country's YMCAs) Naismith's name appeared on an article about "Basket Ball," with a brief explanation of the rules, strategy, and equipment. He also underscored the need for physical directors to keep an eye out for rough play, suggesting that in its short lifetime basketball had already become a contact sport. Almost immediately, the game was taken up in more than 200 YMCAs around the United States. Naismith's original students formed their own team, and played other teams at the Springfield Y and a few outside teams, and they reportedly went undefeated.

Then as now, most of the action at YMCAs took place in the afternoons and evenings, when members—mostly young professional men—left their jobs and came to the Y for a workout. They thought basketball was just great, and would typically play a game with two 15-minute halves after warming up for an hour or so with calisthenics and weight training. The size of the basket was generally determined by what kind of baskets were lying around, and the height of the goal depended on the height of the balcony. When a soccer ball was not available, a football was substituted, and in those first early years basketball was sometimes referred to as "indoor football," because its season so closely followed football's. In fact, some people called successful shots "touchdowns."

By the spring of 1892 thousands of young men were playing basketball, although few, it seems, were playing it well. The development of technique and strategy was hampered by more than just the newness of the game. Part of the problem stemmed from the fact that sides ranged from 3 to 40 players, depending on how many people wanted to play. In games where teams had 10 or more players a side, the poor referee had no chance of seeing every foul, and the pushing and shoving often escalated into wrestling and punching. Indeed, basketball often looked more like "basket-brawl."

As Naismith and other YMCA physical directors watched basketball develop, the need for putting a little space between the players became clear. After some experimentation, men's teams were finally fixed at five players a side in 1897. Among the other important developments during basketball's first five years was the invention of an iron rim 15 inches in diameter, with a rope net underneath. When a basket was scored, the referee would pull a cord that cinched up the net, causing the ball to pop out. Before this invention, an official would either climb up a ladder to retrieve the ball or poke it out with a long stick. The creation of a ball specifically for the sport came about in 1894. The first official basketball was around four inches larger in diameter than a soccer ball, which made it just a little bit bigger than the basketball used today.

Shooting technique in the 1890s was limited to two-handed set shots, with little backspin on the ball. The basketball's laces—similar to those on a football—were quite pronounced, and if they happened to hit the rim the ball could go anywhere. The ideal shot was actually one which had less than one rotation, kind of like a knuckleball in baseball. Occasionally, players would attempt one-handed scoops or finger rolls, but only when they were right under the basket; one-handed play of any kind would be frowned upon for many years to come. Once backboards were introduced, a popular strategy was to fling the ball in the general vicinity of the basket and hope a teammate could grab the ball on the rebound and find a shot a little closer to the basket.

The earliest form of dribbling also began to evolve prior to the turn of the century. The rules of the time stated that a player could not move while he had possession of the basketball. To get around this restriction, a player might throw or roll the ball a short distance and then outrace the defender and pick it up. A tricky player might apply backspin or side spin and go to the spot he knew it would end up. Another popular trick was to toss the ball up just a few inches and move quickly while the ball was in the air—sort of upside-down dribbling. Since the ball technically was not in a player's possession, he could go wherever he wanted. Some of the more coordinated athletes could time the tossing of the ball with each new step and "dribble" the length of the court without the ball ever touching the hardwood! This got to be such a problem that a rule was added which stated that the ball had to touch the floor to be considered "out of a player's possession." Although this new rule eliminated running with the ball, it created a new problem. A team would give the ball to its largest player, who would back his opponent toward the basket a few inches at time, bounc-

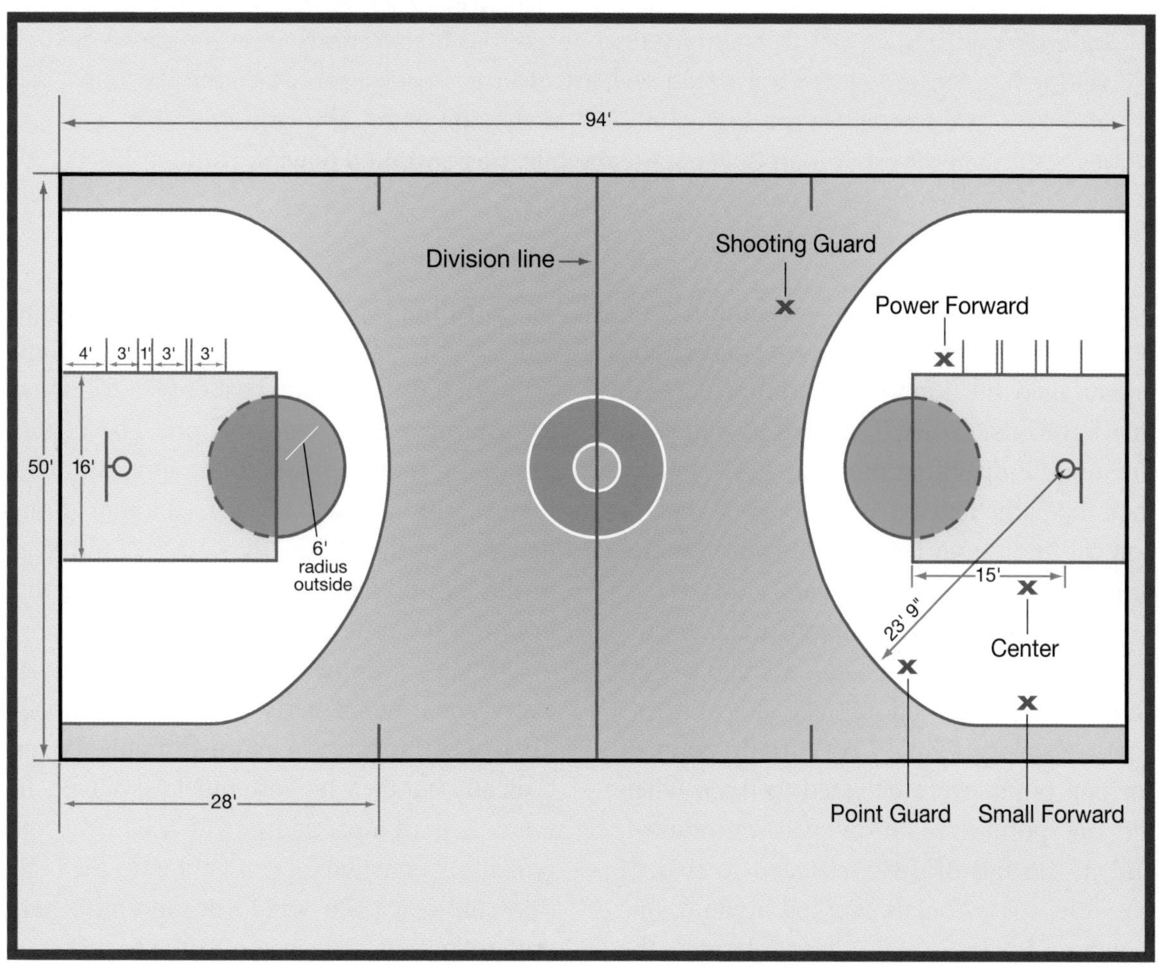

THE ORIGINAL DR. J

James Naismith is usually depicted as a highly moral, educated man from a rock-solid background. The real story is a little bit different. He came from a Ca nadian family that saw more than its fair share of hard times. Born in the province of Ontario on November 6, 1861, Naismith moved east with his family in 1869 to the neighboring province of Quebec when his father purchased a sawmill. A year later, fire destroyed the mill and a typhoid epidemic claimed both of his parents. Nine-year-old James and his two siblings moved in with an uncle, and he grew up plowing fields, chopping wood, and doing other heavy chores expected of a growing boy during this time.

At the age of 15, Naismith dropped out of school and started spending his time in logging camps. For five years he drank, swore, and caroused with the coarse, thuggish lumberjacks. By the time he reached 20, though, he realized quite correctly that he was headed nowhere. Naismith reentered high school, took on extra courses, and graduated at 22. He enrolled at McGill University, where he studied to become a Presbyterian minister. At McGill, Naismith discovered that the strength and stamina he developed as a wood-cutter translated well into sports, and he soon became the finest athlete in the school. He graduated in 1887 at the age of 25, and continued his studies at Canada's Presbyterian College. Meanwhile, he continued playing contact sports,

ing the ball each time and catching it with both hands. It slowed the game down and encouraged the kind of swarming defense that led to fist fights. The YMCA outlawed this double-dribbling move in 1898, but by then the game had expanded beyond the Y's control and some leagues allowed double-dribbling for many more years.

Free throws replaced expulsion for fouls and, for nearly 30 years, a team's best shooter was allowed to take all of these shots. Baskets, which had initially counted for one point, were elevated to three when the one-point free throw was introduced, and in the fall of 1895 reduced to two. If possible, two officials worked a game, one watching for fouls and other violations, the other ruling on possession whenever the ball went out-of-bounds and handling jump-ball duties. Each basket was followed by a jump ball at center court. The center jump, in fact, remained the predominant feature of basketball for another four decades. In the 1890s, the center could leap in the air and catch the ball himself; he did not have to tap it to a teammate.

Defense was the deciding factor in almost every game in the early years of basketball. To make things even more difficult, teams typically put their biggest, quickest players in the defensive area, and they draped over opponents even when they did not have the ball. Sometimes a team would go an entire half without getting a clean shot at the basket.

including professional lacrosse for the Montreal Shamrocks. What an odd fellow he must have seemed to his fellow seminary students.

It was at Presbyterian College that Naismith became convinced that a great way to promote Christianity was by promoting physical activity. The obvious place to pursue this goal was in the United States, where the YMCA curriculum of social welfare and bible study was already being enhanced by an ambitious program of athletics. He was accepted as a student at the Springfield Y in 1890, and asked to stay on as an instructor in 1891 when he completed the Y's one-year physical-fitness course. At the YMCA he played center for the football team, and is credited with coming up with one of the first helmets, which was basically a pair of ear flaps hanging from a flannel headband. It was this knack for invention that made Dr. Gulick believe Naismith might be able to cook up a brand new sport.

Naismith left Springfield in 1895 and moved to Colorado. There he served as the physical director of the Denver YMCA while attending Gross Medical College. He graduated in 1898 and accepted a position as chapel director and professor of physical education at the University of Kansas. He taught basketball to his students for a few years, and served somewhat reluctantly as the school's coach, then kind of drifted away from the game and let others take over. Although he was regularly honored in the press and in person, he never fully appreciated the sport he himself had invented. Naismith died in November of 1939, the first year the NCAA Tournament was held.

The First Pros

One of the YMCA teams that began playing its games outside the YMCA was in Trenton, New Jersey. A group of young men had formed the team there a year after James Naismith invented the game, and they had become quite good at it. By the spring of 1896 they had become so proficient that none of the other YMCA or college teams in the area could beat them. But apparently, housing the champions of basketball was more than any of the other Y members could stand. They monopolized gym time, and no doubt intimidated other members when they did not get their way. So in the fall of 1896 they departed the Trenton YMCA and started playing at the nearby Masonic Temple.

The 10-man Trenton Basketball Team was headed by Fred Cooper and Albert Bratton, while the team's finances were handled by a couple of local sports enthusiasts named Fred Padderatz and W. S. Saunderson. The team paid for its own uniforms, equipment, travel expenses, and practice locations. They negotiated for playing venues, charged for admission, and players received a cut of the gate. In other words, the Trenton club was a professional operation. Cooper, 21, had come to America as a boy and become one of New Jersey's best soccer players. He met Bratton, another fine soccer player, at the YMCA and they both joined the basketball team. These

OFF-COURT ACTION

When a ball went out-of-bounds in the early days of basketball, the rules governing this situation were very clear: whoever retrieved it was awarded possession. This was one of Naismith's more impractical rules, as it created skirmishes in the stands so wild that they made the on-court fisticuffs seem tame by comparison. This was the reason most spectators chose to remain up in the gallery rather than sit at courtside. If a ball went up into the balcony, teams had to quickly choose between sending a man out of the gym and up a staircase, or hoisting a teammate high enough so he could pull himself up and over the railing. When a ball rolled down a staircase, several players would go barreling after it—anyone coming up the stairs at these times was in mortal danger. In short, one was never entirely removed from the action when attending an early basketball game.

Nor was one entirely a spectator. When play spilled into the stands around the court, it was not unusual for a fan of the home team to prevent an opposing player from getting the ball. On inbounds plays, they sometimes pinched or poked opponents with walking sticks. During the winter of 1895–96 the first backboards came into wide use—not to enhance scoring but to prevent spectators from leaning over the balcony railing to deflect enemy shots with umbrellas.

Basketball at this time was also a very rough game. Even highly organized contests with experienced referees were interrupted regularly by bloody noses and fistfights. Throwing a hip or elbow was considered a foul, and players were not allowed to hold opponents; however, many defensive tactics that would be unacceptable today were considered legal during the first decade of organized ball. Contact made body-to-body, for instance, was okay—a defender could get right up in his

two worked together marvelously, using the short passing techniques of soccer to revolutionize the game of basketball. Working 10 to 15 feet apart they would run the floor, passing the ball back and forth as they raced past bewildered opponents. They often beat entire teams with this play, and regularly brought the crowd to its feet.

Was the Trenton Basketball Team the first professional club? It appears so. Other squads no doubt played for money, but rarely expected or received more than enough to cover their travel costs. When one YMCA team played another, for example, admission was charged and the players were reimbursed for their expenses, with the rest going into YMCA coffers. Certainly, some of the better players got a few dollars slipped to them on the side. But not until Trenton (which billed itself as "national champion") man's face with their chests touching, or drape himself over his man's back. Contact with the hands was not considered a foul if, in the referee's opinion, a player was going for the ball. Thus in loosely officiated games, a player could expect to get hacked or slapped every time he touched the ball. If a player happened to be dribbling the ball out in front of him, it was perfectly legal to crash into his arms and separate him from the ball—or even to hit him head-on. As long as the defender made a play on the ball the referees let the game continue. When two players had their hands on the ball at the same time, every man on the floor would join them within seconds to try to get possession. Several times a game, in fact, possession was decided by an old-fashioned tug-of-war.

The Trenton-Brooklyn game in 1896 marked the debut of the cage. This device, constructed by Fred Padderatz, was nothing more than chicken wire or some other meshlike material nailed to two-by-fours to form a 12-foot-high, see-through wall around the court. Although it sounds like some bizarre, uncivilized invention of professional wrestling, the cage was actually meant to ensure that spectators—who paid up to 50 cents to attend such games—could enjoy a civilized evening. The rule giving possession of a ball flung out-of-bounds to the first team retrieving it was still in effect. No one would pay good money for courtside seats if they ran the risk of ending up at the bottom of a pile of sweaty ballplayers. The cage also kept the game moving along, as it was virtually impossible for the ball to go out-of-bounds.

A few teams copied this idea, with some using netting hung from wires. As a rule, these teams played in the East and were independent basketball clubs. A basketball fan at the turn of the century would not expect to find this type of barrier at a YMCA, high-school, or college game. Thanks to the rough, fast-paced brand of basketball played by the early pro teams, a lot of people compared them to monkeys in a cage. Others called them "cagers," a term that lasted for decades after the cage was permanently retired in the 1930s.

took out an advertisement promoting its season-opening game in the autumn of 1896 against the Brooklyn YMCA (billed as "champions of New York") did the first truly professional team begin play.

More than 600 spectators paid between 15 and 25 cents to attend this event. Padderatz, a carpenter by trade, constructed bleachers so that everyone had a fine view. What they saw was the Trenton players, wearing blazing red uniforms, sink the drably attired Brooklynites by a score of 16-1. Cooper was high man with three baskets, and the visitors did not score until they made a foul shot in the waning moments of the game. The contest was a seven-on-seven affair, with both teams using a 2-3-2 configuration that essentially created five-on-five play at both ends of the court. The Trenton players, who probably earned between $5 and $15 each for the game, then hosted a dinner in honor of Brooklyn at a local restaurant.

Trenton continued to dominate opponents during the winter of 1896–97, losing just once to the YMCA team in Millville, New Jersey. They avenged this defeat with a 14-0 victory over Millville in a return match at Trenton, and finished the year with a 19–1 record. One of those wins came against the fellows who had replaced them as the Trenton YMCA's team, and it had to have been a satisfying one.

The Trenton Basketball Team provided a spark for professional basketball, as it soon became commonplace for the best players to get compensated for their appearances. Even some YMCAs were offering to cover the annual dues for top players if they agreed to join the Y team. They had to—more and more, the Y teams found themselves up against superior opponents, many of whom were paying their best performers. The Amateur Athletic Union—which governed virtually all nonprofessional sports in the United States—frowned upon this practice, but permitted amateur teams like those from the YMCA to play against professional ones. The organization was actually more concerned about professional players invading the amateur ranks, and most of the rules it passed were focused on this area. The AAU position on this point was clear: once you had been paid to play basketball, you could never be on an amateur team again.

This rule was interpreted in a number of different ways. Perhaps the most noteworthy was the stance taken by the 23rd Street YMCA in New York City. In 1897, the AAU held its first national basketball tournament and the team from this gymnasium won the gold medal. Believing they could make a living playing exhibition matches against other top teams in the area, the players declared themselves professionals and dutifully informed the AAU. Before they knew what hit them, their YMCA memberships were revoked and they were banned from using the 23rd Street gymnasium. Unfazed, they practiced and played wherever they could, and rechristened themselves the "Wanderers." Over the next decade, they developed a reputation as one of the best teams in America.

The Wanderers made about $10 a man per game, playing a game or two a week in cities close to major railways so they could return to their regular day jobs. The Wanderers did make extended road trips over the holidays and once they played four games in a 24-hour period. They also were the first basketball players to be paid for endorsing a commercial product. In 1901, each player was paid $5 to say he used Hood's tonic. Interestingly, the Wanderers were often mocked by their opponents for "selling out."

In 1898, the first pro basketball league was formed. It called itself the National Basketball League and its six teams were located in and around Philadelphia and Trenton. A minimum salary of $3.75 a week was established (the season ran 20 weeks), and any player caught playing for more than one team was suspended. By season's end only four teams were left and Trenton, as expected, won the championship. The league lasted five more years, with various teams coming and going. Trenton won the title again in 1900, and the Wanderers captured the NBL crown in 1901. By 1902 a few other pro leagues had been formed, but the NBL proved itself superior when its champion, the Bristol club from Pennsylva-

SNEAKS

The ability to make quick stops and starts has always been a key part of success in basketball. At first, this was not very easy. Players used standard gymnasium footwear—high-top leather shoes with soft leather bottoms. Needless to say, there was much slipping and sliding. Tennis sneakers, which offered a little more traction, came into favor by the mid-1890s.

But not until the first decade of the 20th century was footwear being designed specifically for the game of basketball. Canvas high-tops with textured rubber bottoms proved the most successful, and a pair could be ordered from a catalog for between $1 and $5. This basic construction remained essentially unchanged for 60 years, and even in the mid-1970s many pros still wore basic canvas and rubber models on their feet.

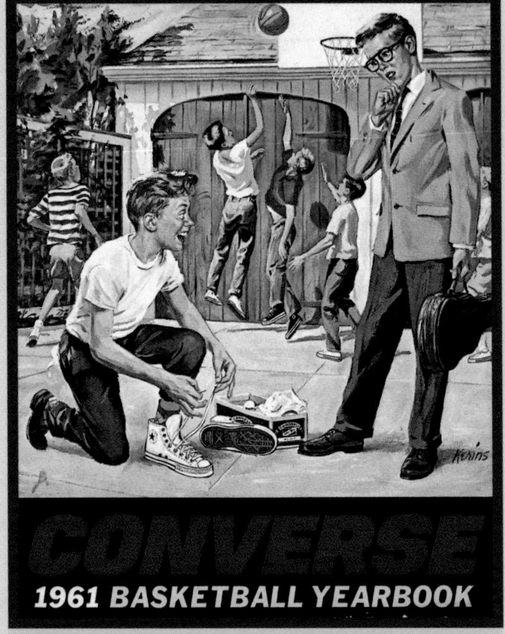

The canvas high-top shoe first appeared on basketball courts in the early 20th century, and reigned as the standard ballplayer's footwear for more than 60 years.

nia, defeated two other league champions in a special tournament.

Although professional teams were springing up all over the Northeast, the era of the full-time pro basketball player was still many years away. Teams usually divided the money generated by ticket sales, so if foul weather kept attendance low the payday would be very disappointing. A well-known team like the Wanderers might receive a guaranteed minimum, but most simply took their chances that a good crowd would show up.

The Pro Game Grows

Thanks to the professional teams in the East, basketball started to become a little more sophisticated around the turn of the century. By this time the accepted number of players was five to a side, which meant that there was more room to move around. The snappy passing of the Trenton club had quickly become the standard means of advancing the ball, and many teams were stationing a man near the foul line with his back to the basket when they gained possession of the ball. He served as the "pivot" for the offense. Passes

THE GERMANS

The first professional team to gain a measure of national fame was the Buffalo Germans. It grew out of the boys' team at the Buffalo YMCA under the direction of Fred Bukhardt, who had been one of Dr. Naismith's pupils in Springfield. From 1895 to 1901, these youngsters were practically unbeatable, and in 1901 they came to prominence during the Pan-American Exposition in Buffalo. That summer the AAU decided to stage all of its annual athletic championships at the fair, including basketball. The Germans, whose members were at this point in their late teens, demolished seven other clubs to win the AAU title. On the tournament's final day, several members of the team had to take school exams and the semifinal game started with just three boys against five. This trio held its own until joined by two teammates, and the team went on to register an inspiring victory.

Over the next few years the Germans got older, bigger, stronger, and more experienced. They entered the basketball tournament at the 1904 Olympics in St. Louis, Missouri (recognized by some historians as the first true national championship), and dominated their opponents by scores of 78-6, 87-35, 97-8, 38-29, and 39-28. They returned to Buffalo as heroes, declared themselves world champions, and began touring as a professional team that winter. Playing with just six men, the Germans went 69–16 against opponents from the Midwest to the Northeast. They continued to barnstorm for many years. The Germans generally stayed close to home, playing teams in New York and Pennsylvania, and once won 111 games in a row.

The Buffalo Germans were the most famous team in the country, but were they the best? Probably not. They generally played weak clubs in small towns, and often lost to teams from big cities. They were, however, a remarkably long-lived organization. Several members of the 1901 team were still playing during the 1910s, and a few sons of the original Germans played on the team during the 1920s.

would go into him and he would hold the ball while his teammates criss-crossed trying to get open. The center jump was also becoming more important. No longer a simple battle for possession, it often set into motion a preplanned offensive play. Because a jump ball followed each basket, a team with a tall center could monopolize the ball and blow an opponent right out of the gym.

During the first two decades of the 20th century, no fewer than a dozen pro leagues were in operation. Some lasted only a year or two, and none managed to stay in business for more than six or seven seasons. Those still operating when World War I began fell victim to the fact that the nation's armories—a prime venue for basketball games—suddenly had to be used to store ammunition and machinery, and were no longer being rented out to pro teams. The most ambitious professional organization during the prewar era was the Central League, which scheduled as many as 72 games a season and operated in the Pittsburgh area. One thousand spectators a night could be found at many of the Central League games.

A big reason for the Central League's success was the willingness of its teams to bid for the best eastern talent. This spending pattern had already been established by the football clubs in the area, and the towns in western Pennsylvania liked the recognition that came from being the epicenter of fall and winter professional sports. Unfortunately, this gave the top basketball players the bright idea that they might sell their services to the highest-bidding team in several leagues at once. It was not unusual, in fact, for a star to wear four or five different uniforms during the same season. This eventually killed the Central League.

Pro basketball's first big star was Eddie Wachter, a 6'1" center with excellent all-around skills. He had something rare in those days: a massive upper body, which he built through sculling on the Hudson River near his hometown of Troy, New York. Wachter was the first basketball player to be sold from one team to another, when at the age of 20 he went from Ware of the Western Massachusetts League to Haverhill in the New England League. For the 1904–05 season he returned to New York and joined his brother, Lew, on the Company E team of the Schenectady National Guard. Also on the squad were two other top players, Bill Hardman and Jimmy Williamson. Company E quickly established itself as the best team in the region, and that spring Wachter and his teammates defeated the Kansas City Blue Diamonds, the top team in the Midwest, in three straight games. After one of the victories, Dr. James Naismith visited Wachter and his teammates in their dressing room and told them that they played the game precisely the way he had meant it to be played when he dreamed it up more than a decade earlier.

In 1909, Wachter and his pals formed the nucleus of the Troy Trojans and joined the Hudson River League. The Trojans were the finest team of the prewar era. Rounding out the squad were Andy Suils, the team's defensive "stopper," and Jack Inglis, the first player whose dribbling and passing skills actually approached modern standards. The Troy Trojans were the biggest

Muscular big man Ed Wachter was the centerpiece of the powerful Troy Trojans, and the first true star of professional basketball.

draw in an otherwise shaky league, often attracting more than 3,000 fans to their games. After two championship seasons in the HRL, they joined the rival New York State League and won its first two league titles. In all, the Trojans reigned supreme in pro basketball for about 10 years. The Wachters, Williamson, and Hardman were the heart of the squad for years, so one can easily imagine how well the team (nicknamed "Wachter's Wonders") played together as a group. They made the bounce pass into a lethal weapon, and pioneered the use of a switching, man-to-man defense that both conserved energy and confused opponents. Wachter was always at or near the top of his league in scoring. He was quick and aggressive near the basket, but also possessed a surprising outside shot. Wachter also initiated Troy's killer play: a long tap from the center jump to criss-crossing teammates, which often resulted in an easy layup. Wachter remained a top player into the 1920s, and became an influential coach for such institutions as Williams College and Harvard University—despite never having attended high school!

Although Wachter was the best-known player of his time, the most important individual in pro basketball during these early years was Frank Basloe. The Hungarian-born entrepreneur grew up in the 1890s throwing a rag ball through the top of a barrel, and his love affair with basketball continued right on up through adulthood. Basloe organized his first pro team at the age of 16 in upstate New York. He scheduled a handful of games with other clubs in the area, recruited four other teenagers—including Lew Wachter and Jimmy Williamson—and turned a handsome profit in his first season. Over the next two decades, Basloe backed a pro team almost every season, and he had some good ones. It was his 31st Separate Company squad that put an end to the legendary 111-game winning streak of the Buffalo Germans. After that game Basloe boldly billed his team as the world champions, enabling him to draw huge crowds to the 100-plus games he scheduled each year. Known at times as the Oswego Indians or Globe Trotters, the team played and beat the finest squads in the country, including many of the strong teams that were beginning to pop up in the Midwest. He would play anyone anywhere as long as he was guaranteed $100 for showing up. This policy brought high-quality hoops to fans in some of the most remote regions of the eastern United States, and kindled an interest in basketball that ignited during the 1920s and 1930s.

Basloe was a brilliant promoter, rarely missing an opportunity to stir up interest or make a few extra dollars. One year he ordered special uniforms that could be turned inside-out to reveal the name of a different team. This enabled Basloe to bring his boys through an area twice without the fans realizing they were paying to see the same team again. When he saw a big crowd, he sometimes tried to incite bad behavior, egging the fans on until they tossed garbage on the floor. Then he would demand more money to keep his team on the court under such dangerous conditions. On the rare occasions when his Globe Trotters were beaten, Basloe would offer the winning captain the team's "World Champions" banner with great sadness and humility. Of course, the other team had to "reimburse" him the $50 that the banner had cost, which they gladly did. Little did opponents know that he had a trunk full of these five-dollar flags.

College Basketball Takes Root

While the professional game struggled to organize itself, the country's colleges and universities were having no such problems. In 1895, a few colleges fielded teams and participated in YMCA competitions against Y teams, local clubs, and even other colleges. Though strictly unofficial, it appears that the first five-a-side intercollegiate game took place in January of 1896 between the University of Chicago and the University of Iowa. The first official game between two schools occurred a year later, when Yale University defeated the University of Pennsylvania, 32-10. Yale was the first team to travel out of its region, scheduling many games in the Midwest, where the University of Minnesota was an influential school.

The first college-basketball leagues were the Intercollegiate League (with Harvard and the other future "Ivy League" universities), the New England League (with Amherst College, Holy Cross, and other smaller private schools), the Western Conference (including Minnesota, Wisconsin, Michigan, and other future Big Ten schools), and the Southern Intercollegiate Athletic Association (led by Auburn University, Tulane University, the University of Georgia, and Georgia Tech). Each was formed during the first five years of the new century. In 1904, the first "College Basket Ball Championship" was held at the 1904 Olympics, right after the Buffalo Germans won the open tournament. Three colleges—Hiram College, Wheaton College, and Latter Day Saints University (later to become Brigham Young)—participated, with Hiram taking the gold medal. The very first Spalding Basketball Guide, published in 1905, correctly predicted that this competition would one day lead to a true intercollegiate basketball tournament, with the championship game to be held in a different part of the country each year.

During the 1904–05 season the two best teams from the Midwest, Wisconsin and Minnesota, traveled east to challenge Columbia University, which was in the midst of a two-year unbeaten streak. Columbia won both contests and claimed what was really the first national college-basketball championship. The following year Dartmouth traveled south from New Hampshire to defeat Yale, Columbia, Manhattan College, and Princeton University, then beat Williams College in a home-and-home series. Yale also made two important southern tours, playing against Auburn, Tulane, Georgia, Georgia Tech, Howard College, Vanderbilt University, and Mercer College. These visits from well-known colleges did wonders for the spread of basketball. Coaches and players shared the techniques and plays they had developed, and occasionally fans got to see big-name athletes who were nationally known for their exploits on the football and baseball fields. Intercollegiate competition, one must remember, was still very much a novelty, as the majority of games during the early years of college basketball were not played against other colleges, but against local YMCA squads, athletic clubs, semipro teams, and even high-school teams. Having a school like Yale drop by for a game was a very big deal.

During the first few years of the 20th century, more than 100 colleges organized basketball teams and played regular schedules. And it was in university gymnasiums that basketball took some subtle but important early steps. Dribbling had become an important part of the college game, and this made play much more physically strenuous. When passing was the sole means of moving the ball, players tended to operate in a limited area of the court. As dribbling techniques became more sophisticated, a single player might advance the ball the length of the court, meaning he and his man might have to run back and forth at full speed several times a game. The average American adult male at this time simply was not in good enough shape to do this, so in many YMCAs and athletic clubs it was agreed that dribbling would be discouraged. However, in colleges—where the players were younger and in far better physical condition—dribbling was encouraged.

Perhaps the most significant aspect of college basketball in the years prior to World War I was the development of coaching. On the professional, semipro, and club levels, a team might have a captain, but he was chosen either for his skills as a player, maker of schedules, or businessperson. In college, the concept of someone who would stand on the sidelines and analyze games and practices gained great support. Fifteen years after Dr. Naismith invented basketball, about half the college teams in America had coaches. By and large, these teams were more successful than those with captains or managers. Because strategies and techniques were still developing at a rapid pace, there was good reason to have someone who could be an objective observer. During the heat of battle, even the smartest player might miss something that a coach would pick up at courtside. Some colleges hired star players who had graduated, some hired active professional players, and some simply added coaching to the normal duties of existing instructors. Each type of coach brought something a little different to the game, and they built upon the work of each other.

The best coach of the prewar era was most likely Joseph Raycroft of the University of Chicago. His teams were up-to-date in all of the latest strategies and techniques, and his players knew how to close out games when they were ahead. In the early 1900s, most college teams had their biggest man stay back and guard the basket, and stationed their best shooter at the opposite end. In other words, most of the back-and-forth action was three-on-three. Raycroft had his big man trail the play down the floor, and had his best shooter and ball handler come back on defense. Raycroft went against the common wisdom of the time, hoping to draw other teams into a five-man game that he knew his Maroons were trained to win. He was able to do so because his biggest player, John Schommer, also happened to be his best.

Schommer was a magnificent athlete, even by modern standards. He stood 6'3" and weighed a rock-solid 190 pounds. Schommer's best sports were football and track. He was an all-conference end for Amos Alonzo Stagg's football team, and he was invited to join the U.S. Olympic track-and-field team for the 1908 Olympics. Schommer declined because the games would have interrupted his studies. On the basketball court, he moved with grace, quickness, and speed, and he did not wither when play got rough under the basket. A graduate of the Central YMCA High School in Chicago, Schommer quite literally grew up on basketball and had a keen understanding of the game. He led the Western Conference in scoring his final three seasons on the team, and earned All-America honors four times. As a defender, he was unparalleled—during one nine-game stretch, he held opposing centers to just four baskets! Schommer's strength and anticipation enabled him to deny his man the ball, and his iron grip helped him haul down every rebound he could get his hands on. In 1908, his incredible last-second basket—launched from an estimated 80 feet away—gave Chicago the national title. After graduation, Schommer obtained a degree in Chemical Engineering and lived a fascinating dual life as an educator and college basketball and football official. He even found time to invent the modern backboard.

John Schommer was the top player in college basketball when he led the University of Chicago to a national title in 1908. He stayed involved in the game throughout his life as an official with the Big 10 conference.

The first coach to take a team without a big star and mold it into a champion was Walter ("Doc") Meanwell of the University of Wisconsin. In his first season, 1912, Wisconsin won all 15 of its games. Meanwell's theory was to control the basketball on offense with a lot of carefully choreographed movement and short, safe passes. Every so often a player would fake toward the ball and then break toward the basket. If he was open, a teammate would pass him the ball for a layup. This simple plan worked wonders: after three seasons Meanwell's squad was 44–1 and he was being hailed as the greatest basketball mind in the country. Only when other coaches began copying Wisconsin's system did his teams suffer an occasional loss.

This sudden "revolution" in offense was met almost immediately by a new defensive tactic: the zone. By spreading five defenders across the court and assigning each a specific area of responsibility, a coach could ensure that his players would not be lured out of position by trickery or sudden breaks to the basket. Instead of actively going after the ball and applying constant man-to-man pressure, defenses now waited for opponents to come to them. Zones cut down on the number of layups and increased the value of a good outside shooter, although "good" back then meant making one out of every three shots. This new defensive strategy also made players start to think more seriously about dribbling, which was still a controversial aspect of the game. Indeed, as coaches became more and more influential in college basketball and began to form their own committees and organizations, the question of whether to abolish dribbling was a major flash point. Many wanted to get rid of it, claiming it was a loophole in the rules and never meant to be a part of basketball. Many more, however, saw dribbling for what it was—the key to basketball's evolution into an exciting, wide-open sport.

THE FIRST COLLEGE STARS

With scoring low and meaningful statistics hard to come by, the top players from college basketball's infancy do not seem impressive by today's standards. And given the way the game was played and who was playing it, no one had the ability to dominate a game the way modern stars do. Still, a few names stand out as the country's best from that era. If John Schommer was the best of the best, then the best of the rest was Christian Steinmetz of the University of Wisconsin. A phenomenal high-school player in Milwaukee, he led his team to a pair of state championships before moving on to star in college. In 1905, Steinmetz personally outscored all of Wisconsin's opponents 462-429, and by the time he graduated he was the first college player to amass 1,000 career points. Steinmetz once hit 20 baskets in a game, and he tallied 50 points in another contest.

At a time when most *teams* struggled to score 20 points a game, Christian Steinmetz averaged a remarkable 25.7 points per contest during his University of Wisconsin career.

Another bright light during the formative days of college hoops was Schommer's teammate, Pat Page. Schommer and the 5'9" Page—a terrific shooter and solid defender—originated the two-man game, which remains a basketball staple to this day. In coach Raycroft's system, Page was the guy who came back, took the outlet pass, and then pushed the ball back up the floor. In that respect, he stands as the first modern guard. Page was daring and unpredictable, and these qualities helped make him the most effective all-around player of his time. He also happened to make two of the greatest shots in college history. In 1908, Chicago and Wisconsin were tied for first place in the Western Conference with seven victories apiece. A playoff was scheduled to determine the champion, who would then travel east to play Pennsylvania. With the score tied 16-16 and time running out, Page was unable to get the ball to Schommer and was too far from the basket to attempt a decent shot. In desperation Page flung the ball high in the air, through a series of steel support girders, and right through the hoop to win the WC title. In the subsequent game against Penn, he was surrounded by three defenders who played him so closely that he could not even straighten up. Fearing the referee would call a time violation, he snapped the ball between his legs like a football center toward Schommer. It sailed over the center's head and right into the basket. After being honored as national Player of the Year as a senior in 1909–10, Page turned down offers from baseball's Cubs and White Sox to pitch professionally and chose instead to succeed Raycroft as University of Chicago's basketball coach.

Although the zone defense slowed down college basketball somewhat, it also forced coaches to think about a lot of things they had ignored during basketball's first 25 years. For starters, it began a long and intensive search for a way to consistently crack the zone—and that meant breaking the game down and studying it scientifically. Basketball's best minds began to see how teammates related to one another on defense, where the weaknesses were, and how to exploit those weaknesses with improved offensive techniques and strategies. These advances were, in turn, met by improvements in team defensive play, which were then analyzed and probed with even newer offensive approaches.

Ironically, the widespread use of zones forced coaches to come up with better man-to-man defensive play. When a team was behind and time running out, it could not continue to play a zone; it had to go after the basketball and cause a turnover. Coaches began devising elaborate double-teaming schemes and sophisticated plays that would leave a ball handler trapped in a corner, or trick a player into throwing an ill-advised pass. A team that could suddenly go from a zone to a man-to-man defense stood a very good chance of flustering its opponent and getting the ball back. These defenses, of course, were easily beaten by players who could think quickly and whip the ball to an open teammate, and thus the value of passing skills and the ability to "see the court" was greatly enhanced as well. Slowly but surely, college basketball was becoming much more sophisticated. As the 1920s approached, the game was about halfway between "Naismith-ball" and where it is today.

Pro Ball in the 1920s: The Reign of the Original Celtics

The end of World War I triggered an enchanting period in American sports. People had more time, more money, and more enthusiasm for athletes and athletic events than at any time in the country's history. Stars who might have enjoyed limited stature in a previous era, were embraced by the nation as demigods, and their every move was covered in great detail on the sports pages, in news reels, and on radio. Babe Ruth was the leading sports hero of this time, but he shared the ever-widening spotlight with Red Grange, Bill Tilden, swimmer Gertrude Ederle, Jack Dempsey, Bobby Jones, and a number of other world-class performers.

Although no basketball players achieved this exalted status between the Great War and the Great Depression, professional basketball itself did benefit immensely from the sports-mad mood in America. Several pro leagues started up after the war, the strongest of which was the Metropolitan League, which pulled together the most popular teams from New York City, New Jersey, and upstate New York.

The most prominent team of the 1920s was the Original Celtics. The Celtics had been in operation as the New York Celtics in the years leading up to World War I, but disbanded in 1916. In the fall of 1918 the team was re-formed by sports promoter Jim Furey. Joining prewar stars Johnny Whitty and Pete Barry on the Celtics were Ernie Reich, Dutch Denhart, Swede Grimstead, and Johnny Beckman. By 1921 the Celtics were regarded as one of the top pro squads in the east. Grimstead played the pivot, with

Dehnert starring on defense and assuming most of the ballhandling duties. Beckman, the best shooter in the game, played forward and provided inspirational leadership with his aggressive and highly vocal approach.

As the Celtics grew in popularity, accounts of their exploits began appearing in New York–area newspapers. This was a first for pro basketball, which had for years been treated badly by sportswriters. With heightened awareness of the Celtics came more attention for other top teams, most notably the New York Whirlwinds, who boasted Barney Sedran, the first college star to play in the pros. The Whirlwinds also had forward Nat Holman, who was the finest all-around player of the early 1920s, and Chris Leonard, who was tall enough to jump center, yet nimble enough to play guard. The team was run by fight promoter Tex Rickard, who believed pro basketball could become a big-time sport. In the spring of 1921 these two teams met for a scheduled three-game series. The first contest, which went to the Whirlwinds, drew more than 11,000 fans. The second game, attended by more than 8,000, went to the Celtics. This created enormous anticipation for a third meeting. Unfortunately, the rubber game never was played. Rumors of attempts by gamblers to fix the contest dampened fan enthusiasm, and two weeks later Leonard and Holman decided to play for the Celtics the following season.

In 1922, after briefly competing in two organized leagues, the Celtics decided to take their show on the road and play as an independent club. They traveled across the eastern half of the country and played a remarkable 205 games between September

The 1923 Original Celtics team, barnstorming champions of professional basketball. From left to right, Johnny Beckman, John Whitty, Nat Holman, Pete Barry, and Chris Leonard.

and April, losing only 11. More than 500,000 fans watched them play, and every team they faced learned something new about the game. It is hard to say how important this road trip was in the overall scheme of professional basketball, but it did establish the Celtics as America's first pro basketball team with a substantial national following. Among the more interesting teams the Celtics played were the all-Jewish Philadelphia Sphas (South Philadelphia Hebrew Association), the all-Irish Brooklyn Visitations, and the best outfit in the Midwest, the Cleveland Rosenblums, who represented a department store in that city. The best team they played was the Kingston Colonials, who competed independently and also in a couple of leagues, all at the same time.

Nat Holman was a top pro as a forward on the great Original Celtics teams of the 1920s, and later rose to the top of the coaching profession at New York's City College.

In 1923, 6'5" Joe Lapchick joined the team. A great leaper, he won the center taps after each basket, meaning the Celtics maintained possession of the ball for long stretches. Lapchick was a good shooter and passer, and was highly coordinated—something that was still considered quite unusual for a man his size. His presence made the team nearly unbeatable. Even so, the Celtic players were under strict instructions never to blow out an opponent. They wanted to make sure fans came out to see them the next time they came through town.

To keep his team together, Jim Furey had to pay his players well. But the Celtics consistently drew big crowds, especially after the new Madison Square Garden opened in 1925. The players were quite well known by basketball fans, even outside the New York area, and they made very good money—as much as $10,000 a year. And they were not adverse to making a little bit more. Once in a while, if an unexpectedly big crowd showed up, the Celtics would let the game end in a tie, then demand more money to play an overtime period, which the poor promoter had to pay in order to avoid being torn to pieces by irate fans. Ironically, all this time it was assumed that Furey was making a handsome profit. Perhaps he was, but if so he proved incapable of handling money. In 1926, it was discovered that he had embezzled nearly $200,000 from his place of business and he ended up in Sing-Sing prison.

In the winter of 1925–26, the American Basketball League played its first season. The brainchild of National Football League commissioner Joe Carr, the ABL was pro basketball's first attempt to "go national."

THE RENAISSANCE

During the 1920s the cultural and commercial nerve center of black America was Harlem, in New York City. The area was undergoing what many called a renaissance, and it both attracted and produced many famous authors, poets, artists, and musicians. One of the many success stories from this era was William Roche, who came from Monserrat and founded an important realty company in Harlem. In 1922, he built the Harlem Renaissance Casino. The first floor was a movie theater; the second floor was a gigantic banquet hall that could be rented for concerts, dances, political gatherings, and other major events.

In the fall of 1923, Roche was approached

The Harlem Renaissance, the first great all-black basketball team. Founder Robert L. Douglas is pictured in the inset.

Carr selected the best teams in the country and invited them to represent their respective cities in a nine-team circuit that stretched from New York and Boston all the way to Chicago. Teams had to sign players to exclusive contracts (like the Celtic players, they could not appear for anyone else during the season) and had to play at least two games a week against ABL opponents. Carr did allow ABL teams to schedule exhibition games, which was still necessary to generate enough revenue to keep a pro team afloat.

The ABL's 32-game schedule was divided into two halves, with the winner of each half meeting in a championship series. The Brooklyn Arcadians club won the first half to earn a crack at second-half winner, the Cleveland Rosenblums. The first two games of the series drew enormous crowds in Cleveland, but only a few thousand showed up when the series moved to Brooklyn. The Arcadians were swept by Cleveland 4–0. The league's leading scorers were Rusty Saunders and Ray Kennedy of Washington, which finished second in both halves of the season.

On the balance, the ABL's first season appeared to be a success. The only real sour note for the ABL was that the exhibition by Bob Douglas, a fellow West Indian from the island of St. Kitts. Douglas, who was well known as a proponent of organized sports for black athletes in New York, asked Roche if he could use the upstairs ballroom for basketball games on Sunday nights. Douglas offered to call his team the Renaissance to give Roche some free advertising, and explained that he would operate the all-black team as an independent unit, playing most of its games on the road. Roche agreed, and the Rens as their fans called them, began their long history with a 28–22 win over the Chicago Collegians (an all-white team) on November 30.

The original five Rens were Leon Monde, Hy Monte, Zack Anderson, Frank Forbes, and Fats Jenkins. They featured snappy passing and suffocating defense, and by game's end their opponents were dog tired just trying to keep up with them. Teamwork was the gospel Douglas preached, and it served the Rens well. Within a couple of years, they were playing at a level comparable to that of the top teams in the east. They often played against the Original Celtics and Philadelphia Sphas, and they won as often as they lost. In later years they began traveling around the country, and even made forays into the South, where they popularized basketball among black students at colleges and high schools.

Douglas rightly went down in history as the father of black basketball. He was a big reason why segregation in basketball never really took hold. As the leading black team in the United States, the Rens always played hard and played clean and exciting ball. Douglas was respected and admired for the way he ran the team and dealt with his fellow promoters, two of whom—Eddie Gottlieb and Joe Lapchick—would go on to play enormous roles in the evolution of basketball.

games scheduled between its teams and the Original Celtics were all humiliating blowouts. This embarrassment was erased the following year when the Celtics agreed to join the ABL five games into the season, replacing the Arcadians, who had failed to draw fans after selling off their best players. The Celtics won 32 of the remaining 37 games and swept Cleveland in the championship. The Celtics repeated as ABL champs in 1927–28, and then went bankrupt. The players were making too much money, and the Celtics were making too little.

By the time the 1929–30 season got underway, the stock market had crashed and the nation's economy had begun to crumble. Like most business people, the ABL owners believed that the setback was only temporary, and went ahead as planned with their season. Attendance dwindled as the economy grew worse, and several teams were in financial ruin by the end of the year. To its credit, the American Basketball League did stay alive for one more season, and actually reorganized a couple of years later. But it was strictly a minor-league operation at this point, with teams limited largely to the New York metropolitan area. However, it did survive in this form right through World War II, and supplied many of the players who helped form the leagues that would one day merge into the National Basketball Association. The ABL was a great idea, but its timing could not have been worse.

Surviving the Great Depression

Professional basketball did not die during the 1930s. It survived in a form very similar to its early days, with regional leagues and semipro circuits offering fans of the sport a decent game at a fair price. Sometimes, that price included a dance or a concert. Indeed, it was not unusual for the building to be cleared and quickly converted into a dance floor after the final whistle sounded. The Depression also gave rise to industrial leagues, especially in the Midwest. A college basketball star in the 1930s would have been insane to turn pro. Instead, he could get a steady job at one of the many manufacturing plants in the country's midsection in exchange for playing on the company team. The combination of a regular paycheck and some small measure of celebrity was enough to lure the top players of the era to these teams, which were technically amateur outfits. Their games were quite competitive and very popular, for fans could actually root for their own company and coworkers.

Between the industrial leagues and the small minor-league circuits of the 1930s, there were enough quality opponents to support a few barnstorming teams. The Celtics sprang to life again and toured on and off throughout the decade, trading on their name and glorious past. They accepted small guarantees, and hoped that fans would come to see their aging stars. They did manage to dig up some new talent, with college stars Polly Birch and Bobby McDermott (history's best two-handed shooter) joining the team. It must have been an odd sight to watch basketball's greatest players pile into a single car and go from one town to the next. And it must have been frustrating to be a Celtic during these lean years. The players split up between $125 and $200 a game; a few years earlier, these same players had commanded salaries of $7,000 to $10,000 each. That is how hard the Depression hit pro basketball.

What kept the Celtics going under these humiliating conditions was the knowledge that they could leave their mark on the game for future generations. Wherever they played, college and high-school coaches would scrape up a few dollars and bring their teams to watch the way the veterans worked the ball on offense and how they switched off so effortlessly on defense. Not until 1940 did the Celtics finally break up for good.

Some of the other top traveling teams of the era were the New York Jewels, which featured some of the players from the powerful St. John's University team of the late 1920s, and the Philadelphia Sphas, who played in the scaled-down ABL and also hit the road with a good deal of success. Eddie Gottlieb, who had coached the Philadelphia Warriors in the heyday of the ABL, built the all-Jewish Sphas into a tight, crisp-playing unit thanks to standouts Inky Lautman, Red Wolfe, Shikey Gotthofer, Moe Goldman, and Harry Litwak. In Chicago, promoter Abe Saperstein had formed an all-black team at the end of the 1920s, which he dubbed the Harlem Globetrotters. The talent level on the Globetrotters, who toured primarily west of the Mississippi, was as high as any independent team in the country, and they usually beat the top industrial-league and minor-league clubs they played .

The most successful barnstorming outfit during the 1930s was Bob Douglas's New York Rens. From 1932 to 1936 they played more than 100 games a year and fashioned a record of 473–49. Fats Jenkins and Bill Yancey—respectively, the team's best ball handler and defender—also barnstormed in the summers, as members of the New York Black Yankees baseball team. The best shooter on the Rens was Bruiser Saitch, who was one of the top black tennis players of his era. This caliber of athleticism was what made the Rens so attractive to audiences both black and white. They played the game at a faster pace than anyone else in the 1930s, and began to explore some of the vertical aspects of basketball thanks to the jumping ability of their players. During one stretch the Rens won 88 straight games. All along, the Rens adhered to Douglas's theories on teamwork, and eventually this style produced behind-the-back and no-look passes that were both entertaining to watch and highly effective.

Douglas had a good thing going and did not want the Rens to grow old together, so a few years later he began bringing new players onto the squad. By the late-1930s, the Rens were completely remade. Douglas was a clever man. He knew how to condition, motivate, and—if need be—replace his players. Each fall he would hold a combination tryout and training camp. The best black players would come from all around and play against the established Renaissance veterans. This got his stars into shape quickly, and gave him a chance to spot new talent on the rise under game conditions. Douglas also invested in a fancy bus that enabled the Rens to travel whenever and wherever they wanted without worrying about finding a hotel that would accept the black players. Each spring the team would travel south to play the best black colleges and club teams. In most states south of the Mason-Dixon line, the Rens were not allowed to play white teams, but up north this was no problem. Even though they regularly pounded white teams, they were always invited back. Being beaten by the Rens was not a disgrace, but actually something of an honor. That is how good they were.

In 1939, the *Chicago Herald-American* sponsored the World Tournament of Basketball, a championship event that would last until 1948. The Rens won the first tournament and were crowned kings of professional basketball. In 1940, they lost in the quarterfinals to the Globetrotters, who went on to win the championship. These two victories clearly demonstrated that black players were every bit as good as white players, and went a long way toward opening the professional game to blacks during and after World War II.

College Ball Between the Wars

It remains one of the most intriguing paradoxes in sports history that, while professional basketball flourished in the 1920s and nearly died in the 1930s, the college game struggled to find its identity during the 1920s only to explode onto the national scene during the Depression. Did one have something to do with the other? It appears that this was the case.

The pros lived, traveled, and worked together—and played three or more games a week—and they were able to master the in-

POP GATES

The star shooting guard of the Harlem Rens teams of the late 1930s and 1940s, William "Pop" Gates.

During the glory days of the New York Rens, Pop Gates was the team's top player. He grew up playing basketball at the Harlem YMCA, just a few blocks away from the Renaissance Ballroom. Although he led Benjamin Franklin High School to the public-school basketball title, he was more renowned in Harlem as a stickball player. But there was not much future in stickball, so he decided to swap his hoops skills for an education. He and the other graduating starters from Franklin accepted scholarships to Clark College in Atlanta, Georgia. But he came back to New York after experiencing the hard racism of the Deep South.

Gates, a shooting guard, led the Rens into battle in the late 1930s and 1940s, and was the leading scorer on the team that won the first World Tournament in 1939. In 1943, when the Rens suspended operations for a time, he joined the barnstorming Washington Bears and led that team to the title at the World Tournament. Finally, as player-coach of the 1947–48 Rens, he hit for 16 points against the Minneapolis Lakers in the last World Tournament final, as his team barely dropped a 75-71 decision.

Gates could have been a tremendously significant figure in the NBA had luck broken his way. When the Dayton franchise of the National Basketball League folded a month into the 1948–49 season, the Rens were invited to take their place and play out the schedule. Although Gates played well and coached the team to a winning record, an all-black team replacing an all-white one in Dayton, Ohio, did not draw very well, and Bob Douglas decided to relinquish the franchise. A short time later, the NBL was absorbed completely into the National Basketball Association, with every franchise coming aboard intact. Imagine how history might have changed had Gates and black stars Nat Clifton, George Crowe, and Duke Cumberland been one of the league's original NBA franchises.

tricate ball-movement offenses that made the game so exciting to watch. The vast majority of college teams, at least for most of the 1920s, were assembled from whatever a school's student body happened to produce. To expect young men with more important things on their minds to knit together into a cohesive five-player unit was unreasonable, especially when one considers that many colleges did not yet have a full-time basketball coach. If the pros looked like "monkeys in a cage" during the early 1920s, college players sometimes just looked like monkeys. This began to change during the 1920s, as coaches grew in stature and influence. By the 1930s, colleges were taking their basketball programs a lot more seriously, and college players finally started to get serious about basketball.

James Naismith led the Kansas University team for many years, although he considered himself more of an instructor than a coach. He always found it amusing that his game required any "coaching" at all. Yet it was one of his students, Forrest ("Phog") Allen, who looked at a basketball court and saw a battlefield crying out for a general. To Allen basketball was a game that, even more than football and baseball, could be influenced by the man on the sideline. After bouncing around for a few years after graduation, Allen ended up as the coach at Kansas in 1919, and for the next two decades he and Naismith coexisted on the same campus. This could not have been easy—Naismith probably thought Allen was wasting his life, while Allen clearly believed the good doctor had no appreciation for this wonderful sport he had created.

Allen was a dictator who believed in training, conditioning, a good diet, and massive water consumption. He also was a superb and creative motivator who was not above spinning an elaborate yarn to get his players fired up. Allen also devised a defensive strategy still in use today when he taught his players to shift from a basic zone to a tight-checking man-to-man and then back to a basic zone. This totally confused opponents who liked to run different plays against the two different types of defenses. In 1922 and 1923 Allen's teams were the best in the country, and the Jayhawks either won or tied for the conference title 15 times in the years between the wars. During that time Allen became the nation's foremost recruiter and a vocal supporter of the coaching fraternity.

The zone-defense principles developed during the teens were polished during the 1920s thanks to coaches such as Notre Dame's George Keogan, who came up with the moving zone when he arrived in South Bend in 1924. Keogan had his two best rebounders flank the basket and more or less stay put, but encouraged his three perimeter defenders to apply intense man-to-man pressure and gamble in the passing lanes. When dribblers ran them into picks and screens, they would bounce back into position and let a teammate on the other side pick up the man with the ball. This made penetration difficult, and took its toll on an opponent's outside shooters during the course of a game. If a team did manage to pass inside against Notre Dame, the shooter

Forrest ("Phog") Allen learned the game straight from James Naismith. He succeeded Naismith as coach at Kansas University, and helped to define the role of the modern college-basketball coach.

paid the price as the Irish baseliners were instructed by Keogan to allow no easy baskets. In two decades at Notre Dame, Keogan went 327–97 despite playing an ambitious schedule against many of the best schools in the country.

With defenses getting more and more complex during the 1920s, the offensive approach of many coaches was to grab a quick lead and then play an opponent to a stalemate the rest of the way. The problem with this theory was that, if you did not have the offensive players to score those early baskets and grab that lead, you were in trouble. The first person to attack this dilemma with any success was coach Doc Carlson of the University of Pittsburgh. During a 1927 game versus Army, the solution suddenly came to him, and he dubbed it the "continuity" offense. Two players stood their ground, while the other three weaved through the zone in a figure-eight pattern, stretching the defense out of shape with every pass. With the ball passed crisply with each rotation, eventually a man would get open—either popping out to the perimeter or establishing position inside for an entry pass. From this basic play, Carlson could flood one side of the zone and set a screen or pick for his shooter, or send a dribbler slicing in from the wing with the option of shooting or passing, depending how the zone reacted. One way or another, the defense was bound to make a mistake with cutters swirling all around them, and the Pittsburgh players worked this system beautifully.

Initially, Carlson's system was looked upon suspiciously, for he had Chuck Hyatt, a multitalented 6' forward perfectly suited to make it work. Pitt had the best team in the land in 1928 and 1930, but the true test of the continuity offense came in 1931 after Hyatt graduated: The system—without any star players—won 24 games. Within a couple of seasons, everyone was working on a continuity offense, with some involving four or five players in constant motion.

While most coaches spent the 1920s tinkering with ways to foil the zone, Ward "Piggy" Lambert discovered a way to score before it even had a chance to set up. The Purdue University coach got the idea when he looked at his Boilermaker squad in the early 1920s and saw an interesting combination of players. His captain, forward Ray Miller, was an excellent defensive rebounder who could also dribble and pass the ball. His center, Blair Gullion, was not as strong on the boards, but ran the floor quite well for a big man. Lambert suited up himself during practices and started working out a system where three or four of his players would break down the floor the instant they saw Miller positioning himself to rebound a missed shot. The captain would whip the ball to his nearest teammate, who would push it up the court and try to take advantage of a mismatch or numbers advantage for an easy basket.

Purdue used this "fast break" approach with fairly good success for several years until, in 1928, Lambert was able to assemble an ideal group of players to make his idea work. Stretch Murphy, a 6'6" center and dominant rebounder, would clear the ball out to Lloyd Kemmer, a great passer and ball handler. The Boilermakers began scoring 40 and more regularly—an impressive total in an era when many games still saw both teams combine for 40. In 1929–30, high school star Johnny Wooden joined the team and transformed Purdue into an unbeatable squad. Wooden could push the ball up on the break or finish it with a twisting layup, but his biggest contribution came on the defensive end, where his anticipation and stamina effectively neutralized an opponent's top scorer. Wooden made All-America three straight seasons, and combined with center Ralph Parmenter and forward Harry Kellar to form the nucleus of a team that went 42–8 over three seasons. After Wooden graduated, the Lambert break continued to win, capturing five conference titles between 1934 and 1940.

The man who brought the fast break to the big arenas in the East was the University of Rhode Island's Frank Keaney, who adopted this style of play during the mid-1920s. Keaney's system began with defense: The team's best rebounder stayed close to the basket while his four teammates harassed, trapped, and otherwise exhausted their men. Then they would sprint the other way on offense—often trying long, risky passes. By game's end URI opponents were so tired that the Rams would cut them to ribbons, and in no time at all the team had crashed the point-a-minute barrier. Toward the end of the 1930s, Keaney's offense was rolling up 70 points or more a game. Naturally, by this time almost every college team could run a fast-break offense if conditions warranted. This was a vital development in the college game, for it forced players to hone their open-court dribbling and passing skills, and put a premium on the ability to handle passes on the dead run.

Long before John Wooden became a coaching legend at UCLA, he was the heart of the Purdue University Boilermakers of the early 1930s, history's first fast-breaking team.

College Basketball in New York

By the mid-1920s, the New York City metropolitan area had been the center of the tiny pro-basketball universe for more than two decades, but it hardly qualified as a hotbed of college ball. All of the game's progress after World War I had been made in other parts of the country, and as late as the fall of 1927 the region had yet to produce a college team with any kind of national reputation. Prior to the war, the only basketball New Yorkers knew was what they saw the professionals play. This disciplined and highly organized style of play was impossible for untutored college kids to copy, especially when they were not exposed to good coaching.

Things began to change during the 1920s, when several colleges hired men with pro experience—including Nat Holman of the Celtics—to guide their teams. Progress, however, came slowly because New York colleges almost never traveled outside of the area. New York players, in fact, were largely unaware of all of the trends developing in the South, West, and Midwest. So they stuck to the intricate, quick-passing Celtic style, and eventually several colleges actually mastered it.

The first top team belonged to Fordham University, which lost just four games in three seasons between 1926 and 1929. The school that got all the attention, however, was St. John's University. Coach Buck Freeman handpicked five of the best local high-school players and brought them into his program together as freshmen. Center Matty Begovich stood 6'5" and could jump, which gave the Redmen total command of the center tap. Forward Mack Posnack was the most talented passer in the country and guard Mac Kinsbrunner ranked among the games best dribblers. Allie Schuckman, the other guard, had an accurate shot and a lightning-quick release. Freeman was the first coach to do advanced scouting of opponents and study the moves of the key players, and he would devise special defensive plans for each opponent. These defensive attacks were spearheaded by Rip Gerson, whose quick hands earned him the honor of guarding the other team's top scorer. From 1927–28 to 1930–31, the "Wonder Five" went 86–8 and played a key role in the explosive popularity of college basketball in New York City.

By this point, Fordham, St. John's, and several other city teams had large and enthusiastic followings. And just about every college—big and small—had a team good enough to knock off anyone else in the city. That is how high the quality of play had risen by the early 1930s. New York was totally turned on by college basketball, and the Celtic style was being played with great skill and effectiveness all over New York.

Ironically, officials at New York's colleges did not embrace their basketball programs. With the exception of Fordham, which had a 2,500-seat gymnasium, no other school could accommodate the crowds clamoring to see their games. Time and again fans had to be turned away. Every so often a promoter would put up the money to rent a ballroom or small armory and do some advertising. The result, without fail, was a large and enthusiastic turnout.

It seemed obvious to everyone that New Yorkers had a huge appetite for college basketball, and more importantly they were eager to fork over their hard-earned Depression dollars to watch the top schools play. Yet only Ned Irish, a sportswriter for the *New York World-Telegram,* had the guts to put up his own money to stage big basketball events. During the 1920s Irish had become convinced that basketball could become a major-league sport, and he noticed a direct correlation between the amount of buildup he gave a game in print and the number of fans who showed up to see it. By the mid-1930s, Irish had gained enough stature and made enough money to contract with Madison Square Garden for five dates during the 1934–35 season. He quit his job at the paper and threw himself into arranging and promoting these events, which featured the top local teams against famous schools from around the country. The first doubleheader Irish promoted saw NYU play Notre Dame and St. John's take on Westminster, a small Pennsylvania college whose team featured Wes Bennett, the game's top center. More than 16,000 fans attended the event, putting enough cash in Irish's pocket and giving him such a good reputation that he became the world's foremost basketball promoter almost overnight.

Promoter Ned Irish staged games between the top college teams of the 1930s at Madison Square Garden and made New York City the center of the college-hoops world.

Irish scheduled a dozen or more college doubleheaders at the Garden, and also put on successful events in Philadelphia and Buffalo—two eastern cities that were a little easier on the travel budgets of financially strapped western schools. Irish also pioneered radio broadcasts of his games, and even tinkered with television. One night he set up a closed-circuit link to several local theaters so that those who were turned away at the gate could still see the games.

Irish's activities also had a direct effect on the level of play in New York City and the outlying areas. Kids could suddenly picture themselves as college basketball stars, and they took up the game from their earliest years. Thus by the end of the decade, metro New York high schools and colleges were stocked with hundreds of quality players.

In 1938, New York proclaimed itself the center of the college basketball universe when local sportswriters staged the National Invitation Tournament at Madison Square Garden. The top teams in the country were invited to play that spring, and Temple University won the inaugural competition. The NIT was the "last straw" for midwestern basketball coaches, who deeply resented the eastward shift of power during the 1930s. In 1939, the National Association of Basketball Coaches—led by Ohio State coach Harold Olsen and a coalition from the Midwest—put on a competing eight-team tournament that pitted the top school in the East against the best of the West. The inaugural event (won by the University of Oregon) was a disaster, drawing a total of just 15,025 fans and sending the NABC deep into debt. The coaches felt very strongly that if a national college tournament were to be held, then the NCAA ought to do it. The NCAA agreed, and took over the tournament the following year, making it college basketball's official championship. The NCAA and NIT events coexisted quite peacefully (with the NIT holding slightly more prestige) into the 1950s, giving college basketball fans the richest and most exciting postseason of any sport. To this day the tournaments remain the two most prestigious events in college basketball, with the NCAA getting top billing and the NIT being less important.

College Stars of the 1920s and 1930s

The years between World War I and World War II saw college basketball go through an era dominated by coaches and coaching strategies. But it was the players who made the baskets and blocked the shots. The ones who stood tallest during the 1920s were Paul Endacott, Vic Hanson, Branch

CLAIR BEE

The most admired college coach of the 1930s was Clair Bee of Long Island University, which played its games in Brooklyn. The Blackbirds went undefeated in 1935–36 and again in 1938–39. During the 1936–37 season, Bee extended his winning streak from the prior season to 43 games. LIU won the National Invitational Tournament in 1939 and 1941, and Bee continued to produce marvelous teams after World War II. He resigned in 1951, after discovering that some of his players had consorted with gamblers. Remembered primarily as the inventor of the 1-3-1 zone defense, he also pioneered the 3-second rule and pushed hard for the 24-second clock after joining the NBA as coach of the Baltimore Bullets. Bee was the most successful coach in New York when that city produced the best basketball in the country. His LIU teams won an astounding 95 percent of their games, even though his best player, Marius Russo, was a better pitcher than basketball player. To this day, Bee's overall career winning percentage of .827 remains the best in history.

Clair Bee and his LIU Blackbirds on the bench during a 1939 game.

McCracken, John Roosma, and Cat Thompson. Endacott learned the game from the master one Saturday morning when Dr. James Naismith was tinkering with some new ideas at the YMCA in Lawrence, Kansas. He went on to become the finest high-school player in the state and then enrolled at Kansas, where he led the Jayhawks to an undefeated season in 1923 under Phog Allen. A great leaper, he often took the center tap though he stood just 5'10". Endacott was probably Naismith's all-time favorite player, and he was good enough to consign a talented backup by the name of Adolph Rupp to the bench for most of his college career.

Hanson was one of the best all-around athletes in the country, and he captained the Syracuse University baseball, football, and basketball teams in the mid-1920s. Though slightly built, he played forward for the Orangemen, who went 48–7 during his three varsity seasons. The 1926–27 squad was the country's finest, and Hanson was generally regarded as the top man in the college game that season. McCracken, who became one of the great coaches of all time at Indiana University, was the school's first great player. He made all-conference at center, guard, and forward in three varsity seasons and led the Hoosiers in scoring each year.

The sharp-shooting Roosma—who gained national fame as a member of the Passaic High "Wonder Team" in New Jersey (which won 159 consecutive games in the early 1920s)—accepted a commission at the United States Military Academy and led the Cadets to 33 wins in a row and an undefeated 1922–23 season. The 6'1" forward's three-year record at Army was 70–3, and he was one of the first collegians to tally 1,000 points in a career. Thompson made headlines as a high-schooler, too. In 1925, his Dixie High team traveled from Utah to play in a national tournament in Chicago. Although Dixie finished second, Thompson, a 5'10" guard, scored 56 points—an amazing total at any level back then. He went on to star for Montana State University, where he provided the scoring for the Golden Bobcats during a three-year run that saw them lose only four games. Thompson made All-American each year, and was hailed as the top marksman in the nation while he played.

The 1930s also saw a number of fine players. Among the biggest names during the decade were Chet Jaworski, Moose Krause, and Paul Nowak. Jaworski was the finisher on the University of Rhode Island fast break when coach Frank Keaney was beginning to build his team into a major power. The 5'11" guard led the nation in scoring in 1937–38 and again the next season. Krause and Nowak were the centers who keyed Notre Dame's moving zone. In coach Keogan's system, they were the anchor men on defense, and played an important passing role in the team's Celtic-style offense. Krause made All-American every year he played for the Fighting Irish, averaging in double figures during the 1932–33 season. Nowak, who came to South Bend and earned All-America laurels from 1936 to 1938, was a menacing 6'6" pivotman who ruled the middle. In his sophomore and junior years, Nowak's team lost just five games and many fans felt—given Notre Dame's tough schedule—that the school was tops in the nation.

The most famous and influential player of all between the wars was Hank Luisetti of Stanford University. Prior to the mid-1930s, a few players had toyed with the idea of shooting with just one hand, but no one had ever had any success with this style.

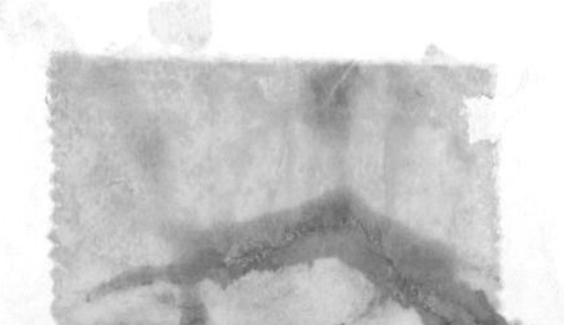

Hank Luisetti perfected the running one-handed shot. The fluid Stanford University star is among the handful of basketball players who can be said to have truly changed the game.

Most coaches, in fact, would not allow anything but two-handed set shots. Luisetti, who grew up in San Francisco, was a tremendously agile athlete. He noticed as a teenager that he could outrun and outleap defenders with relative ease, but it was impossible to throw up an accurate two-hander while moving so quickly. So he began working on a graceful, one-handed push shot which he could fire on the run, either off the backboard or straight into the basket. This was something no one had ever seen before. Soon Luisetti was basketball's first unstoppable player.

By the time he enrolled at Stanford, Luisetti had perfected several variations on his one-hander. He could charge toward the basket, bound into the air and float in a running one-hander from either side. He could also stop quickly, leap straight up and let the ball go as he approached the top of his jump—an early form of the jump shot. Luisetti could also cut through the lane from left to right and curl the ball into the basket with one hand. Or he could take a one-handed set shot if he had the time. Occasionally, he even attempted a jump hook. The Stanford freshman team enjoyed an undefeated season and Luisetti racked up huge point totals.

When Luisetti joined the varsity, the team retooled itself to make the most of the 6'3" forward's dribbling, passing, and shooting skills. The Indians ran the break whenever possible; their half-court offense featured a weave designed to spring Luisetti for slashing drives to the basket. Word of the one-handed wonder reached the East during the 1935–36 season, and Stanford was invited to showcase its star in Madison Square Garden the following fall. The Indians topped Temple University in front of 9,000 fans in Philadelphia, then moved on to New York, where Clair Bee's top-ranked LIU Blackbirds were waiting for them. Nearly 20,000 fans packed the Garden and watched in shock as Luisetti either scored or set up most of Stanford's points in an easy 45-31 win. The victory ended LIU's heralded winning streak at 43, and made Luisetti a national idol. The newspapers made his one-hander sound as mysterious and futuristic as a rocket ship, and much was made of his movie-star good looks. Meanwhile, a legion of imitators sprang up almost overnight, and within a few weeks it seemed everyone in college was fooling around with the one-hander.

Stanford returned to Madison Square Garden a year later to edge Nat Holman's hot-shooting CCNY squad, then ran LIU off the court again. On their return trip west, the Indians played Duquesne University on a neutral court in Cleveland. Luisetti's teammates told him to go to the basket whenever he had a chance, and the result was a 50-point performance and a 92-27 win. He finished his career by winning a third consecutive Pacific Coast championship and earning All-America honors for the third season in a row; he also was named national Player of the Year for the second time. Luisetti had become so popular by the time he graduated that he was offered a movie contract. He made $10,000 to play opposite Betty Grable in *Campus Confessions,* and planned to act a little and play a little ball. But the AAU claimed Luisetti was technically making money from his basketball, and suspended him for a year. Luisetti quit show business, took a job with Phillips 66, and played a few games for the company before blowing out his knee.

The New Big Men: College Ball in the 1940s

World War II barely affected college basketball. Although many players went into the service, most of the tall ones were exempt from the draft because of their height or related medical reasons. Those who did enter the military were replaced by freshmen and transfer students, as rules restricting their participation in varsity games were relaxed. Colleges in densely populated areas went about the business of playing their normal league games, with hardly a change from the prewar years. Schools in more remote areas found this a little more difficult, as a combination of wartime travel restrictions and fuel and rubber shortages made traversing long distances a little tricky at times.

The elimination of the center jump prior to the 1937–38 season produced some radical changes in college basketball, though it was not until the 1940s that its long-range effects started to become clear. The center position had to be rethought completely, for the clumsy and uncoordinated big men who had proved so valuable when a jump ball followed each basket were of no use anymore unless they could do something else. For a while, it looked as if big men would be legislated out of the game. But in the nation's grade schools and high schools, a revolution began to take place. After 1937, whenever a coach got a player who was 6'5" or taller, he began working with him on footwork, passing, dribbling, jumping, and shooting. After a few lean years for centers, a different type of pivot player began to appear on the college scene, and this proved to be the most important development of a very important decade for basketball.

In many ways the first "modern" centers were Bob Kurland and George Mikan. Kurland was a seven-footer whose parents had kept him out of sports for most of his teen years because they were terrified he might injure other boys. Despite the lack of basic athletic skills caused by this deprivation, Kurland did have some natural ability. He won the state high-jump championship as a high-school junior and he spent a lot of time hunting and fishing. Oklahoma A&M coach Hank Iba recognized that Kurland had a lot of untapped potential and offered him a scholarship. The first year in college was

BASKETBALL GOES TO THE OLYMPICS

Although basketball has long been a sport associated with the United States, it has been played with varying degrees of success in dozens of countries around the world. Starting in 1920, the game began appearing on the world stage during the summer Olympics. That year Parisians watched the Americans defeat all comers, as basketball was played as a demonstration sport. Four years later, in Amsterdam, another demonstration tournament was held. Finally, in 1936, basketball was made an official Olympic sport. The first competition, which was held outdoors in Berlin, Germany, nearly set the game back 40 years. The final was played in a driving rain storm and the court became a muddy quagmire, making it impossible to move quickly or dribble. The U.S. beat Canada 19-8.

Mexican and Philippine players battle for a rebound during the 1936 Olympics.

For most of its history, Olympic basketball has been little more than a clinic put on by the U.S. national team. In 1948, the U.S. sent a team made up of the NCAA champion Kentucky Wildcats and the AAU powerhouse Phillips 66ers. As expected, they humiliated their opponents, although a Chinese player did drive to the basket through the legs of seven-footer Bob Kurland. In 1952, the USSR froze the ball in the gold medal game, and stayed within a few baskets of the U.S., but eventually succumbed 36-25 to a team led by Kurland and Clyde Lovellette. Four years later, the Soviets were overwhelmed 89-55 in the final by a team featuring Bill Russell and K.C. Jones. And in 1960, the U.S. sent its strongest team to date, with Jerry West, Oscar Robertson, Jerry Lucas, Walt Bellamy, and Bob Boozer leading the way. They wiped out the Soviets again, 81-57, to win the gold medal.

During the 1960s, as basketball became more sophisticated in the United States and the level of play improved dramatically, the sport was also undergoing a transformation in the Soviet Union. A program to produce a highly skilled, highly trained "amateur" team was set in motion. Athletes were selected at a young age and placed in intense training programs designed to produce veteran players who could compete with the young college stars who made up the U.S. Olympic teams.

By 1972, the USSR had accomplished its goal. In the gold medal final they held a 49-48 lead over the U.S. with just seconds to play. But Russian star Sergei Belov lost the ball to Doug Collins and was forced to foul him, and then Collins calmly sank two free throws to give the U.S. a 50-49 advantage. The Soviets failed to score in the time remaining, and the Americans bounded gleefully off the court, having escaped an embarrassing loss. But according to officials, the game was not over. After some confusion at the scorer's table, it was decided that the Soviet coach had called for a time-out before the ball was put into play, and the USSR was awarded a second chance. A long pass found its way to Belov, who muscled past two defenders to score the most controversial basket in Olympic history. The American players, feeling they had been robbed, refused to accept their silver medals.

In 1976, the U.S. got a scare from Puerto Rico. Butch Lee of Marquette, one of the top players in the nation, was angered at not being allowed to try out for the team, so he joined Puerto Rico, where he had been born. He scored 35 points against the U.S., who barely managed to squeeze out a 95-94 victory. Revenge against the Russians was not possible, however, because a spirited squad from Yugoslavia had beaten them in the semifinals. The U.S. won the gold medal easily. In 1980, with the U.S. boycotting the Olympics, the Yugoslavian team took the gold medal, with the Soviets finishing with a bronze. The 1984 games saw the Soviets boycott, which left the door wide open for college superstars Michael Jordan, Patrick Ewing, Wayman Tisdale, and Chris Mullin to dominate the competition.

In 1988, however, the U.S. was humbled in Seoul, South Korea, as the team led by David Robinson, Mitch Richmond, and Danny Manning failed to reach the final round. The problem was that the young Americans were no match for the seasoned professionals from Communist countries. Their official occupation could be listed as anything from butcher to baker to candlestick maker, but in reality they were paid to do one thing: play basketball. This was becoming a growing problem in other Olympic sports—athletes from the Soviet Union and Eastern Europe technically worked for the government, so even though they were professional athletes, there was little to prevent them from competing in the Olympics as amateurs.

A solution was reached prior to the 1992 Olympics in Barcelona, when it was announced that professionals would be allowed to play in the basketball competition. This brought about the birth of the famous Dream Team, which included Jordan, Ewing, Robinson, Mullin, Larry Bird, Charles Barkley, John Stockton, Scottie Pippen, Karl Malone, Clyde Drexler, Magic Johnson, and Duke University star Christian Laettner. The U.S. easily won the gold and demonstrated basketball at its highest level, spurring a burst of interest in every corner of the globe. Since 1992, the NBA has seen a major influx of foreign-born players, and foreign leagues have actively pursued American players, making basketball a truly international game.

Big George Mikan's towering stature was only one of the attributes that made him basketball's first dominant center. The DePaul University All-American could shoot with either hand and was as coordinated as a much smaller man.

like a science experiment—no one had ever showed Kurland how to shoot, so Iba set about teaching him the hook shot. After missing the rim on his first 200 attempts, the big kid finally began to get the hang of it. In the meantime, he contributed to the Aggies by standing under the basket, where he would leap up and bat away enemy shots just before they went into the basket. This was perfectly legal at the time, but Kurland was so good at "goal tending" that in his junior year the play was outlawed. By then, however, the young man they called "Foothills" had learned how to play position defense and had increased his mobility dramatically. This resulted in back-to-back NCAA championships for the Aggies in 1946 and 1947.

Mikan was a shade smaller, but an altogether different kind of player. He and his father played basketball constantly while he was growing up, and by the time he got to high school he stood nearly six feet tall. A severely broken leg left Mikan bedridden for a year and a half and kept him off the team all four years, during which he grew another eight inches. He decided to enroll at DePaul University in 1942, the same year the Blue Demons hired a new coach named Ray Meyer. The two agreed that Mikan could be an awesome center if he could recapture the skills he had as a boy. Meyer designed an exhausting training regimen which included rope-skipping, shadow boxing, ballet dancing, and about 500 shots a day. Mikan, who was still growing, also played in Chicago's top-flight CYO (Catholic Youth Organization) leagues, where he could hone his game against the city's top black players, including Sweetwater Clifton.

In no time at all, Mikan was the best big man the game had ever seen. He could

WMGM SPORT CALENDAR—DECEMBER 1948

SUNDAY	MONDAY	TUESDAY	WEDNESDAY	THURSDAY	FRIDAY	SATURDAY
THIS CALENDAR PLACED NEAR YOUR RADIO, WILL REMIND YOU TO ENJOY THESE AND OTHER FEATURES OVER NEW YORK'S STATION FOR SPORTS — WMGM, ON THE DIAL AT 1050.			1 PRO BASKETBALL Rochester vs. New York 9:00 P.M.	2 COLLEGE BASKETBALL N. Y. U. vs. Baylor St. John's vs. Penn. 9:00 P.M.	3	4 PRO BASKETBALL Indianapolis vs. New York 2:00 P.M. COLLEGE BASKETBALL C.C.N.Y. vs. Brigham Young L.I.U. vs. Bowling Green 9:00 P.M.
5 FOOTBALL Giants vs. Pittsburgh 2:00 P.M. HOCKEY Rovers vs. Boston 4:45 P.M. Rangers vs. Detroit 9:00 P.M.	6 COLLEGE BASKETBALL N.Y.U. vs. Colgate St. John's vs. Denver 9:00 P.M. BOXING From St. Nicholas Arena following basketball	7 HOCKEY Rangers vs. Bruins 9:00 P.M.	8 PRO BASKETBALL Providence vs. New York 9:00 P.M.	9 COLLEGE BASKETBALL L.I.U. vs. Arkansas C.C.N.Y. vs. S.M.U. 9:00 P.M.	10	11 PRO BASKETBALL Baltimore vs. New York 2:30 P.M. COLLEGE BASKETBALL N.Y.U. vs. Georgetown St. John's vs. R. I. State 9:00 P.M.
12 FOOTBALL Giants vs. Washington 2:00 P.M. HOCKEY Rovers vs. Quebec 4:45 P.M. Rangers vs. Detroit 9:00 P.M.	13 BOXING From St. Nicholas Arena 10:00 P.M.	14 COLLEGE BASKETBALL C.C.N.Y. vs. Brooklyn L.I.U. vs. Okla. A. & M. 9:00 P.M.	15 HOCKEY Rangers vs. Toronto 9:00 P.M.	16 COLLEGE BASKETBALL Manhattan vs. Bradley N.Y.U. vs. Texas 9:00 P.M.	17 COLLEGE BASKETBALL Yale vs. Cornell 8:30 P.M.	18 PRO BASKETBALL St. Louis vs. New York 2:30 P.M. COLLEGE BASKETBALL L.I.U. vs. Kansas State St. John's vs. Kentucky 9:00 P.M.
19 HOUR OF CHAMPIONS 12:30 P.M. HOCKEY Rovers vs. Ottawa 3:30 P.M. Rangers vs. Montreal 9:00 P.M.	20 COLLEGE BASKETBALL N.Y.U. vs. Georgia L.I.U. vs. Georgia Tech 9:00 P.M. BOXING From St. Nicholas Arena following basketball	21 COLLEGE BASKETBALL C.C.N.Y. vs. Oklahoma St. John's vs. Iowa State 9:00 P.M.	22 PRO BASKETBALL Minneapolis vs. New York 9:00 P.M.	23 COLLEGE BASKETBALL N.Y.U. vs. Colorado L.I.U. vs. Butler 9:00 P.M.	24	25 PRO BASKETBALL Chicago vs. New York 9:00 P.M.
26 HOUR OF CHAMPIONS 12:30 P.M. HOCKEY Rovers vs. Sherbrooke 3:30 P.M. Chicago vs. Rangers 9:00 P.M.	27 COLLEGE BASKETBALL N.Y.U. vs. Yale L.I.U. vs. Rice 9:00 P.M. BOXING From St. Nicholas Arena following basketball	28 COLLEGE BASKETBALL C.C.N.Y. vs. Alabama St. John's vs. Utah 9:00 P.M.	29 PRO BASKETBALL Rochester vs. New York 9:00 P.M.	30 COLLEGE BASKETBALL L.I.U. vs. Western Kentucky C.C.N.Y. vs. San Francisco 9:00 P.M.	31 HOCKEY Boston vs. Rangers 9:00 P.M.	

THE SPOT FOR SPORTS IS **1050** ON THE DIAL
(WMGM-FM 100.3 MCS.)

Season's Greetings
May our programs add pleasure to your holidays, and to your listening throughout the New Year.
WMGM

Basketball had become a big-time attraction by the late 1940s, as this broadcast calendar dominated by college and pro basketball games of New York radio station WMGM shows.

shoot with either hand, and he went to the hoop as powerfully as anyone before or since. Three times Mikan was selected as an All-American, and he led the nation in scoring as a junior and senior. Overall, the Blue Demons went 81–9 during Mikan's four years with the varsity. Kurland and Mikan met five times in college, with DePaul winning three games and the Aggies taking two. Kurland played in a slow, conservative system that was perfectly suited for his skills, and was probably the more effective of the two at the college level. Mikan was the focus of his team at both ends of the court, and thus was often asked to do more than he could. Not until he joined the pro ranks would "Big George" find a system that got the most out of his immense ability.

Two other important developments in college ball during the 1940s were the further

Holy Cross star Bob Cousy delivers one of his patented no-look passes. Traditionalists frowned on the flashy, creative playmaker, but Cousy proved at Holy Cross and later with the Boston Celtics that his skills could be the engine of a lethal, and winning, attack.

development of the running game and the rise of the University of Kentucky. The fast break evolved quickly from the basic approach of Piggy Lambert and became quite sophisticated under the tutelage of coach Bill Reinhart of George Washington University in St. Louis, Missouri. Because of the school's second-rate facilities and unambitious scheduling, Reinhart rarely had more than a couple of good players. Yet he always managed to produce a winning team. He trained his boys to move into their offense immediately after a shot went up—an idea now called the "transition" game—in order to gain a numerical advantage when play swung the other way. When a GW player pulled down a defensive rebound, an outlet man would move to a predesignated spot near half-court, while two other teammates raced down the court to create a three-on-two advantage.

Ed Hickey, who left the pro ranks to coach Creighton and then St. Louis University, also used the break with great effectiveness. For three straight seasons beginning in 1940–41, Creighton edged Hank Iba's powerhouse Oklahoma A&M squad for the conference title, and in 1947 Hickey's St. Louis team won the NIT with center Ed Macauley, who could both clear the boards and finish the break. Another coach who adopted the fast break was Branch McCracken of Indiana University, who won the 1940 NCAA title.

The reason so many teams went to the break was because it worked very well when the other team was bigger and taller. A team that played a slow, deliberate offense typically had to be better than its opponent in order to win, but this was not the case with a fast-breaking squad.

It was the fast break, in fact, that brought a championship back to the region that gave birth to basketball. Holy Cross, a team without a starter over 6'4", won the NCAA championship after switching to a fast-break attack early in the 1946–47 season. One of the players on this team, freshman Bob Cousy, would later take control of the Crusader offense and draw the spotlight to a new type of college player: the big guard who could dribble, pass, and score from 20 feet. Other six-footers had blended

SCANDAL!

Kentucky's "Fabulous Five" squad—Alex Groza, Ralph Beard, Kenny Rollins, Wah Wah Jones, and Cliff Barker, along with Coach Adolph Rupp—won an NCAA title and represented the United States in the Olympics. The legacy of the Fabulous Five, however, turned out to be an ugly one. As good a team as they were, it turned out they might have been even better. Groza and company were accused of conspiring with gamblers to "shave" points—purposely scoring less than they could have in order to win games by slim margins. The gamblers would bet that the Wildcats would not defeat their opponents by more than a certain number of points, and Groza and company would make sure not to win by more than that amount.

Technically, they were not throwing games. But sometimes this scheme backfired and Kentucky did lose. These revelations came out during a 1951 investigation that revealed widespread game-fixing in college basketball. In all, 32 players at seven schools were involved. Further investigation turned up other problems, including secret payments by Kentucky to its best players. As punishment, the NCAA shut down the Wildcat basketball program for a year.

When the team resumed play, Rupp continued using the same formula and won his fourth NCAA championship in 1958. But he was never really the same man. Bitter and betrayed, he became known as one of the meanest men in college basketball.

Despite the sanctions slapped on the Kentucky program, the center of the college basketball scandals in 1951 was New York City. Almost overnight, it went from being the undisputed center of the basketball universe to a cesspool of corruption and gambling. Several schools canceled their basketball programs, while the rest had an extremely hard time attracting freshmen recruits. Although the National Invitation Tournament continued to be held, it lost its luster and became a sideshow to the NCAA Tournament—a relationship that remains relatively unchanged to this day. Without its core of nationally ranked local teams, the NIT could no longer put a decent field together. And without top players and a strong NIT field, New York City ceased to be a factor in college basketball.

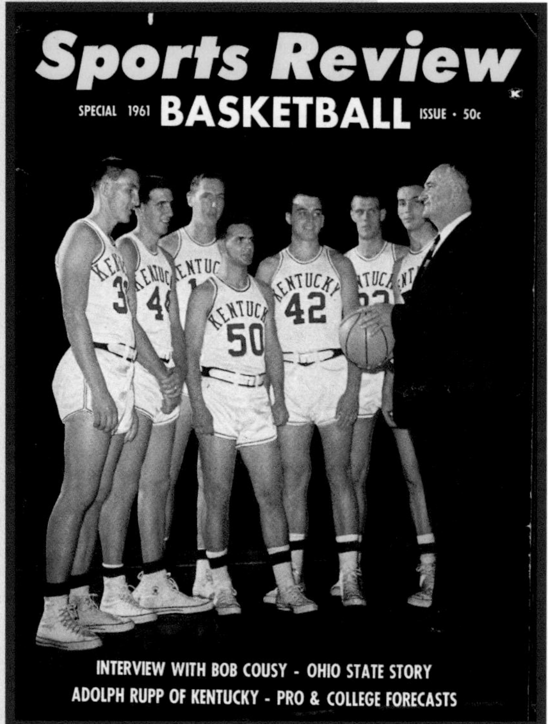

Adolph Rupp and his always-formidable Kentucky Wildcats. Rupp won four national championships and an astonishing 876 games over his 40-year career, but his legend has been tarnished by allegations of racism—Kentucky did not field a black player until 1969—and his harsh treatment of his players.

these skills before Cousy—most notably Bob Davies, Bobby Wanzer, and Dick McGuire—but no one had ever done so with his special flair. Fans would cheer whenever Cousy pulled off his patented behind-the-back dribble, and they went crazy when he would throw no-look passes from his shoetops or over his shoulder. Though he could never lead Holy Cross to another title, Cousy's appeal while he was in college was unprecedented. He brought showmanship and versatility to a sport that was lacking in both departments, and convinced a lot of doubters that the fast break could be run with intelligence and consistency. Indeed, by the beginning of the 1950s, the big debate in college was no longer about which region played the best brand of basketball, it was which style of play was the best: fast break or ball control.

During the latter half of the 1940s, the best college basketball was being played by Adolph Rupp's University of Kentucky Wildcats. He assembled a team that embraced all of the key ideas of the time. His players could play big or run, and could also fulfill more than one role within the team concept. His rebounders could pass, his shooters could dribble, and his low-post defenders could hustle down the court and finish plays under the basket. Schooled in the art of coaching by Phog Allen, Rupp came to Kentucky in 1930 and immediately began scheduling games outside of the region. He drilled his players relentlessly in practices to cut down on errors, and criticized them nonstop—even in victory—to keep them from letting up. If a mistake was made during a game, it meant an immediate seat on the bench.

Rupp may have been tough, but he was also flexible. He designed his offense to make the most of the individual skills of his players, rather than trying to fit his players into a set system. For instance, if a player had a consistent jumper from the right baseline—and the defense was leaving that spot unattended—Rupp would call that play until it stopped working. If a player had an accurate hook coming across the lane from left to right, Rupp would design a play that cleared out any defenders who might pop over and try to double-team the ball. In short, there was not a defense that Rupp could not solve. He would get his players open shots; if they hit those shots, they won every time.

By the mid-1940s Kentucky had become a tough road team with a reputation for knocking off the nation's top schools. In 1943–44, the Wildcats ranked among the best colleges in the country, and in 1944–45 they began a great run when Alex Groza came to Lexington. Groza had hoped to receive a scholarship from Ohio State, where his brother Lou was a star lineman and placekicker for the football team. But no offer was tendered, so he went south and enrolled at Kentucky. The 6'5" center helped the Wildcats win their first 11 games, outdueling Arnie Risen in a satisfying victory over Ohio State.

Unfortunately, Groza was lost to the military for most of that season—and missed the entire 1946–47 campaign—but when he returned in the fall of 1947 Rupp had added a talented bunch of players. Center Wah Wah Jones, guard Ralph Beard, and forward Joe Holland had played marvelously as freshmen in 1945–46, leading the Wildcats to the NIT championship. Groza returned from the military weighing 220 pounds and having grown two inches taller, and Rupp filled out the Kentucky squad with several more nationally known players, including Bob Brannum and Jim Jordan. As expected, the team rolled over its opponents with a combination of fast breaks, outside shooting, and flashy inside play. The dream season ended with the NIT finals, when the Wildcats were ambushed 49-45 by the University of Utah, led by Arnie Ferrin and Vern Gardner.

The following season, Rupp put it all together and created the finest college team to that point in history. After experimenting with different lineup combinations, he settled on Groza at center, Beard and floor general Kenny Rollins at the guards, and Jones and Cliff Barker on the front line. Thus the "Fabulous Five" was born. Each man could shoot well, and as a unit the Kentucky starters were exquisite ball handlers. On defense, Rollins checked the other team's best playmaker, while Groza tied up the center—effectively nullifying the heart of an opponent's attack. Barker was a small ball-handling forward, while Beard was one of the top all-around players in the nation. They bumped off Cousy's Holy Cross team in the semifinals of the NCAA tournament and then beat Baylor University by 16 in the final.

The Fabulous Five went on to represent the United States in the Olympics, joining forces with the five starters (including Bob Kurland) from the Phillips 66ers, the top AAU team. The U.S. swept to a gold medal with eight easy victories in London, culminating in a 65-21 pasting of France in the final.

The following year coach Rupp decided to make Groza the focal point of the offense. The big man not only responded by becoming a super scorer, but the rest of the team also managed to elevate its play. The Wildcats repeated as NCAA champions, with seniors Groza, Beard, and Jones earning All-America honors.

Ancestors of the NBA: The NBL & BAA

During the 1930s, the best basketball players in the land were scattered amongst several different types of teams. Barnstorming clubs were still criss-crossing the country, playing games for a cut of the gate and a small guarantee. Individual businessmen sponsored teams that played against clubs and semipro squads in a region where they hoped to benefit from the name recognition a good team might bring. And several major corporations fielded teams, hiring former college stars as factory employees and then suiting them up for twice-weekly games. In 1935, a group of these teams banded together and formed the Midwest Basketball Conference. The 1935–36 champion was the Chicago Duffy Florals, and the Akron Goodyears took the second MBC flag. In the fall of 1937, the organization changed its name to the National Basketball League to sound more important.

Though strictly a regional phenomenon, the NBL was successful enough in the years prior to World War II to offer attractive contracts to recently graduated All-Americans. Some big-name players made upwards of $300 a week, while average players made $200 to $300 a month. Even that rate of pay, however, was far better than the typical American worker might expect to make—if he had a job at all. Early in the 1941 season, the Japanese bombed Pearl Harbor and America suddenly found itself at war. Although many NBL players were exempt from the draft, over the next year most of the top performers were lost to the military.

THE JUMPER

By the mid-1940s, one-handed shooting was all the rage. This changed the very nature of basketball. Because a one-handed shooter could score on something other than a layup or a wide-open outside shot, teams could run many more plays than in the past. With better offense, though, came better defense. Soon defenders learned how to minimize the damage done by one-handed shooters by playing them very tightly.

Then along came Kenny Sailors. A 5'11" forward for the University of Wyoming, Sailors reasoned that he could get his shot off a lot easier if he held onto it until he reached the apex of his jump, and then transferred all of that energy into the ball with a little flick of the wrist. It was the first real jump shot, and it worked. Sailors averaged 15 points a game during the season and led Wyoming to the 1943 NCAA championship. Sailors actually unveiled the shot during the 1940–41 season; and he claimed to have developed it way back in 1933 while playing against his older, taller brother in their backyard.

Still, the NBL managed to survive. It took a little luck, a lot of hard work, and some important ground-breaking.

The three strongest teams of the war years were two Wisconsin teams—the Sheboygan Redskins and Oshkosh All-Stars—and the Zollner Pistons of Fort Wayne, Indiana. The Redskins were comprised of college stars from the region and although their record was not always stellar, the team did manage to win the NBL championship in 1943. The All-Stars were much more successful, both on the floor and at the gate. The team had a devoted following, and an owner who always went after the best talent available. Players used to performing in front of huge college crowds found the small-town atmosphere of Oshkosh strange at first. But they were treated like kings and paid well for their services.

The Pistons were owned by Fred Zollner, whose plant made a fortune during the war. He spent a great deal of that money supporting his players. Each had a high-paying job (and war-exempt status) at the Zollner Piston Company, and shared in any profits the team made at season's end. This deal attracted some of the finest players of the era to Fort Wayne, including former college stars Blackie Towery, Elmer Gainer, Curly Armstrong, and Herm Schaefer. Also on the team in the 1940s were former Celtic standouts Paul Birch and Bobby McDermott. In the mid-1940s, the Pistons added Buddy Jeanette, perhaps the best-known pro of the war era, and John Pilkington, one of the games most highly prized pivotmen. With this collection of talent, the team won three championships in a row.

Despite paying top dollar for his stars Zollner turned a profit, suggesting for the first time that professional basketball might have a future as a legitimate major-league sport. True to his word, he turned the team's profits over to his players, who made as much as $8,000 each above and beyond their salaries. In many ways, this marked the birth of the modern professional game.

As was the case in the colleges, the biggest change of all during the 1940s was the size of the people playing the game. By the end of World War II, every NBL team had a center who stood 6'6" or taller, and some had two more sitting on the bench. Most of these big men were ungainly and only moderately coordinated, but they were good enough to score when they got the ball around the basket, and quick enough on defense to make basketball's most common scoring play, the layup, far more difficult than it had been in the past.

The 1945–46 season saw dozens of former pro stars return from war, and the NBL

INTEGRATING THE PROS

Faced with choices like filling their rosters with second-rate players or simply folding their franchises, NBL owners did whatever they had to in order to survive during the 1942–43 season. Two teams—the Jim White Chevrolets from Toledo, Ohio, and the Chicago Studebakers—could not even put five decent men on the floor. So they went to the league and asked if they could use black players. The NBL, realizing they would lose these franchises if they refused, agreed to the experiment. Blacks and whites playing on the same floor was not unusual—the Rens, Globetrotters, and other all-black teams often played white opponents. And in many colleges blacks and whites wore the same uniforms (Jackie Robinson had starred on an otherwise white team at UCLA prior to the war). Sid Goldberg, owner of the Jim Whites, selected the four best black players in Toledo: Al Price, Casey Jones, Shannie Barnett, and Zano Wast. Unfortunately, the team folded after just four games. The Chicagoans fared much better. The Studebaker factory had been converted to wartime production, meaning its key employees were exempt from the draft. Among these "key" workers were several former college stars and at least five members of the Harlem Globetrotters. Despite some attempts by the press to stir up trouble, the Studebaker players got along fine, and the fans treated the black players well.

These players were not the first to play in white professional leagues. In 1935, the Buffalo Bisons had 6'4" center Hank Williams on their roster when they joined the Midwest Basketball Conference. In the years prior to World War I, the Mohawk Valley League and Eastern League had a couple of black players. The first to integrate pro ball, however, was a man named Bucky Lew. He played for Newbury of the New England League in 1904 and later played for the Haverhill club.

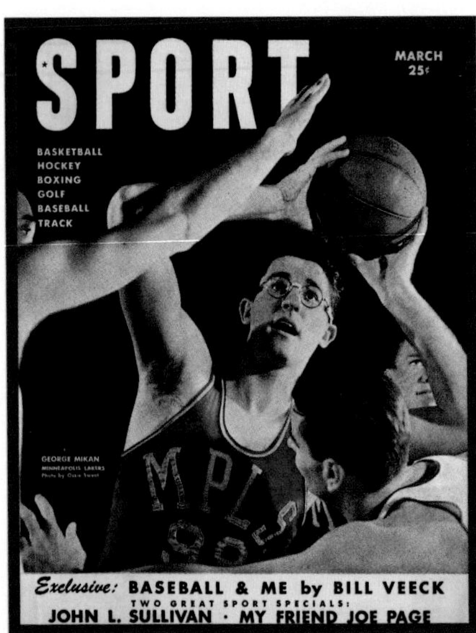

George Mikan was the dominant figure in pro basketball during the latter half of the 1940s and the early 1950s. His nationwide popularity was crucial to the pro game's development as a major-league sport.

even let a couple of new teams into the league. One was the Chicago American Gears, who stunned the sports world by offering DePaul University center George Mikan a financial package worth $60,000 over five years. This was more money than anyone had ever made playing basketball, and Mikan readily accepted. He was in uniform for the team's last seven games, five of which came during the World Tournament in Chicago. The 6'9" Mikan dominated play, scoring 100 points during the competition and earning tourney MVP honors. And thanks to Mikan, for the first time professional basketball was getting a little national attention.

A few months after George Mikan lit up the World Tournament in 1946, the NBL would have its first major competitor. Arena owners in the Midwest and Northeast had long been filling their seats with ice hockey, college basketball, boxing, and wrestling fans. With everyone back from the war they felt that a new pro basketball league might also keep the turnstiles clicking, so they got together and formed one. They called their organization the Basketball Association of America and chose as their president Maurice Podoloff. He was a talented executive who was president of the American Hockey League and operated an arena in New Haven, Connecticut.

To distance themselves from what they considered to be the small-time NBL, each team in this new league was named after the city in which it played, rather than for the company that owned it. Rosters were set at 12 players and a voluntary team salary cap of $55,000 was established. Games were set at 48 minutes—eight minutes longer than everyone else was playing—with four 12 minute quarters. The schedule was 60 games, which was 16 games more than NBL teams played that year. No outside exhibition games—a big money-maker for NBL clubs—would be permitted. Eleven teams competed in the BAA during the 1946–47 season, including the Boston Celtics, New York Knickerbockers, and Philadelphia Warriors. Among the BAA's bench leaders in its inaugural season was a 29-year-old ex-high-school coach named Red Auerbach, who patrolled the sidelines for the Washington Capitals.

The first BAA season was a success on the court. Every team played all of its games, rosters stayed consistent throughout the year, and most of the highly touted stars performed as expected. The Warriors won the league championship thanks to their two star forwards, playmaking Howie Dallmar and high-scoring Joe Fulks. At the gate, the story was not as good. The total revenues fell short of covering player salaries, and every team lost money. Four clubs dropped out of the league at season's end.

Meanwhile, the NBL was doing just fine. The league grew from 8 teams to 12 prior to the 1946–47 season, and because its clubs were less spread out around the country than the BAA's it saved a bundle in traveling expenses. NBL attendance was roughly equal to the BAA's, while player salaries were lower, so several teams managed to turn a profit. Mikan, playing in his first full season, continued to dominate, though he nearly gave NBL owners a collective heart attack when he walked out on his team for a month after Chicago owner Maurice White failed to deliver on portions of his incentive-laden contract. Mikan did return in time to bring the Gears back into

JUMPIN' JOE

The big story in the BAA's first season was Joe Fulks. The former Murray State Teachers College star had played in the Marine Corps during the war, and those who saw him play could hardly believe their eyes. Fulks started a revolution with his jump shot, which he cocked back past his ear and let fly after leaping high in the air. He was not the first player with an accurate jumper, but he was the first player to embrace the idea that a player with great jumping ability could hang in the air until a defender began to come down, and then release a shot unmolested.

After the war the Philadelphia Warriors signed Fulks to a handsome contract and he rewarded owner Eddie Gottlieb by averaging 23.2 points per game and dropping in more than 400 points more than anyone else in the BAA. The Warriors won the BAA championship with ease, as Fulks topped 30 points twice against the outgunned Chicago Stags.

Fulks was definitely a handful. He stood 6'5" and was murder with his back to the basket. "Jumping Joe" could hit hook shots with either hand, and launch his jumper by twisting 180 degrees in the air. In three BAA seasons he averaged more than 23 points per game, and was a star well into his thirties in the NBA with the Warriors.

Joe Fulks, high-scoring star of the Philadelphia Warriors of the late 1940s and early 1950s, was the first player to popularize the jump shot.

the playoff hunt, and led the NBL in scoring with an average of 16.5 points per game.

Despite his holdout, Mikan was immensely popular with the fans. Big George was not a fluid, graceful player—he had only a couple of decent moves. But Mikan was a warrior. Opposing teams would punish him in the post and harass him under the boards, yet he never gave an inch. When he wanted to take the ball to the basket, there was simply no stopping him—never before had a man so big played the game with such intensity. Maurice White believed Mikan's star appeal was great enough to start a whole new league. In 1947, he pulled the Gears out of the NBL and set up the Professional Basketball League of America, with 16 teams. Within a few weeks it was clear that White had made a disastrous miscalculation. The league folded, White lost more than half a million dollars, and his business went bankrupt.

The NBL was glad to be rid of White, and ecstatic to have Big George back. His contract was awarded to the Minneapolis Lakers, who already had one of the game's top players in Jim Pollard. The Lakers were tough to beat with Mikan in the middle and Pollard on the wing, especially after guard Herm Schaefer joined the team from Indianapolis and began feeding them the ball every time down the court. The Lakers beat the Rochester Royals in the finals to win the NBL title.

In the BAA's second season, the going was still very tough. While the NBL expanded its 1947–48 schedule to 60 games, the BAA scaled its slate back to 48, and scheduled doubleheaders to attract more fans. A tight race for the league title helped boost attendance slightly, but the quality of play was nowhere near the NBL's. In fact, the league champion ended up being the Baltimore Bullets, a team that had just joined the BAA from the supposedly inferior American Basketball League. Baltimore's 30-year-old player-coach, Buddy Jeanette, pulled it together for one last run and led his team past the Chicago Stags, the Knicks, and the Warriors to capture the title. For their fine work, the players received a pen and pencil set and celebrated their championship at the local delicatessen—pro basketball had come a long way, but obviously it had a long way yet to go.

Podoloff Makes His Move

Anyone with eyes could have told the difference between the two professional basketball leagues in the spring of 1948. The NBL played in tiny buildings but had the big names, the big crowds, and the most stable franchises. The BAA had less talent, poor attendance, and played in huge, empty arenas. Feeling they had "won the war," many NBL owners became complacent. They did not believe pro hoops would ever outgrow towns like Oshkosh and Sheboygan, and saw no reason to seek a wider audience. The BAA owners, though losing a lot of money, saw the big picture: If pro basketball were to become a national attraction, it would do so in places such as the Boston Garden and Madison Square Garden, and in major markets such as St. Louis, Washington, Philadelphia, and Chicago. The BAA had the quality cities and facilities—all it lacked was the quality product. Toward the end of the 1947–48 season, Maurice Podoloff set in motion a plan to bring the NBL's talent into the BAA. By May the Fort Wayne Zollner Pistons, Minneapolis Lakers, Indianapolis

Kautskys, and Rochester Royals agreed to leave the NBL and join the BAA. The Oshkosh All-Stars and Toledo Jeeps asked to join, too, but they were denied.

The NBL scrambled to replenish its ranks, adding the Hammond Calumet Buccaneers, Waterloo Hawks, Detroit Vagabonds, and Denver Nuggets, an old AAU team that decided to take a chance and go pro. But it was too late. The NBL teams played out the 1948–49 season, with rookie center Dolph Schayes of the Syracuse Nats and veteran big man Don Otten of the Tri-Cities Blackhawks the only decent players left. In July of 1949, a group of NBL owners approached the BAA and waved the white flag, saying they wanted to end the war and work out a merger. In a month the deal was done—every remaining NBL franchise was accepted into the new National Basketball Association.

Although the NBL has generally been pushed aside by NBA historians, it is hard to imagine the NBA succeeding had it not swiped the talent it needed from the older league. For evidence, one need look no further than the first six NBA champions: each title-winner between 1950 and 1955 was an ex-NBL franchise, as was the BAA's 1949 champ, the Minneapolis Lakers. With the passing of the NBL, pro basketball lost the most successful undertaking in its 50-year history. But in order for the pro game to live on, the NBL had to die.

The Decade of Superstars: College Ball in the 1950s

By the mid-1950s, college basketball was undergoing a magnificent transition. Although the game had been evolving steadily during the 1930s, 1940s, and early 1950s, a group of remarkable athletes burst upon the scene. They played a brand of basketball that seemed to be about 20 years ahead of everyone else. They had unlocked the secrets of the game, unleashing a set of modern "vertical" skills on opponents who were still playing a horizontal game. These were players who could create their own shot, no matter how closely they were being guarded. They could put a move on a defender that had him flying out of his socks, then burst to the basket and rise up to the rim for a layup or dunk shot. Although most good high-school players today possess these skills, only a few individuals had them in the college game of the 1950s. And they absolutely destroyed their opponents.

Elgin Baylor, Oscar Robertson, Tom Heinsohn, Bob Pettit, and Jerry West all came onto the college scene between 1954 and 1958, and each unveiled a set of offensive skills that defied any of the conventional defenses. Baylor, who grew up in Washington, D.C., did not pick up a basketball until he was 14 because prior to that the city's public playgrounds were not open to blacks. This probably helped him, for when he did start to play he made up moves as he went along. Baylor could dribble and shoot as well as a guard, and he had a head fake that stopped would-be defenders dead in their tracks. Once he got a step on his man, Baylor could elevate off the floor—either straight up or forward—and get a clear shot at the basket. In other words, anytime he had the ball in his hand, it was basically his decision whether he would drive, pass, or throw up a shot. There was no way to defend him; the opposing team simply had to wait until he made up his mind what he wanted to do. A poor student, Baylor scared off the major

THE GLOBETROTTERS

Lee Garner and Marques Haynes (with ball) of the Harlem Globetrotters. Haynes was the inspiration behind a new generation of slick and creative ballhandlers.

As the 1940s began, the best team on the planet was the Harlem Globetrotters. During the 1930s, while the Rens restricted their travels to the East and South, Abe Saperstein's outfit expanded its territory past the country's midsection all the way to the West Coast and Pacific Northwest. Because the Trotters played in so many small towns, their competition was not very good. To relieve the monotony of winning, and keep the fans coming back, the team worked aspects of its popular pregame clowning into actual games. Although they were not yet known as the "Clown Princes of Basketball," the Globe trotters were developing a reputation for their showmanship and entertainment value. The first player to turn on the crowds with his bag of tricks was Inman Jackson. He could palm the ball in one of his gigantic hands, spin it backwards, and then make it roll up one arm, across the back of his neck, and then down the other.

In 1939, the Globetrotters were invited to compete in the World Tournament in Chicago, where they lost to the Rens in the semifinals. In 1940, the Trotters returned to the World Tournament and beat the Rens in the quarterfinals. In the final, Jackson and company edged the NBL's Chicago Bruins to claim the pro title. Billing themselves as world champs, the Globetrotters began touring the East. Crowds loved their flamboyant spin on legitimate basketball. Unlike most other teams, whose guards did most of the ballhandling, the Globetrotters worked a complex weave

colleges and ended up playing basketball and football for the College of Idaho. But after the school decided to cut back its sports program, Baylor transferred to the University of Seattle, where he led the nation in rebounding in 1956–57 and finished third in scoring. The following season he led tiny Seattle all the way to the NCAA final.

Robertson, a guard, presented college defenses with similar problems. He possessed the ballhandling and passing skills of a point guard, but at 6'5" he towered over most of the players quick enough to guard him. His out-

with their center in the middle and all four remaining players darting back and forth, throwing behind-the-back passes and flipping the ball back and forth with blinding speed.

In 1942, a charming, rubber-faced center named Goose Tatum joined the team. He could work the offense and keep up a constant dialogue with teammates, opponents, and fans. Every so often, he would loop a 25-foot hook shot into the basket, bringing crowds to their feet. He also came up with the fake free-throw idea. Tatum would pull the ball back just as it was about to leave his hands, causing opponents to stumble into the lane and get whistled for violations. Crowds never seemed to get enough of this gag. As the comic heart of the Globetrotters, Tatum was responsible for drawing white fans to the team's games.

In 1943, Marques Haynes joined the club. He was the man who, more than anyone else, got black players interested in basketball. A magical dribbler, Haynes put on spellbinding exhibitions during games, often eluding three and four defenders at once. His blend of showmanship and skill stirred the black athletes of the era, and he became the basketball equivalent of a virtuoso jazz musician. Wherever the Globetrotters played, Haynes captivated the young black fans, while Tatum kept the white fans laughing.

Although they never won another World Championship, the Harlem Globetrotters did beat George Mikan and the Minneapolis Lakers in exhibition contests twice in 1949. When the NBA began taking the best black college players in the 1950s, the Globetrotters had to depend more and more on their reputation as clowns. The novelty of good black players was no longer novel enough to put fans in the seats, so Saperstein worked more and more routines into games. Eventually, the Trotters began touring with their own opponent, whose players were paid to go along with the funny routines. During the 1960s and 1970s, the Globetrotters reached the apex of their popularity. The team was led by Meadowlark Lemon and Curly Neal, who worked sophisticated versions of the routines developed by Tatum and Haynes. By this time, however, any pretense of serious basketball had been abandoned. To this day, however, the Trotters remain the most popular basketball team in the world.

side shot was nearly automatic, but he was even more dangerous when allowed to drive or shoot off the dribble. The "Big O" also rebounded better than most of the centers he faced. He averaged 33.8 points per game in three varsity seasons and set more than a dozen NCAA scoring records.

Heinsohn and Pettit were hot-shooting forwards who could muscle their way inside or pop from the perimeter. Heinsohn, who often played center for Holy Cross, led the Crusaders to the NIT championship in 1954 and an overall record of 67–14 during the three years he was on the varsity. He could drill long jumpers from outside or bull his way to the basket, where he was a smart and aggressive rebounder. Pettit was taller and skinnier than Howell and Heinsohn, but what he lacked in strength he more than made up for with his silky-smooth shooting and driving ability. The 6'9" forward was a two-time All-American at Louisiana State University, and averaged more than 27 points a game during his career.

Jerry West was the hottest high-school recruit in the country in 1956, and could have played at any college in the nation. He chose to stay in his home state and accepted a scholarship from the University of West Virginia. There he rivaled Robertson as the best all-around guard in college, exhibiting shooting, playmaking, and defensive skills that few believed possible. West did not have a single flaw in his game, and he was a tough and talented leader. As a junior, he took the Mountaineers all the way to the NCAA final, and in his senior year West averaged 29.3 points and earned All-America honors for the second straight season.

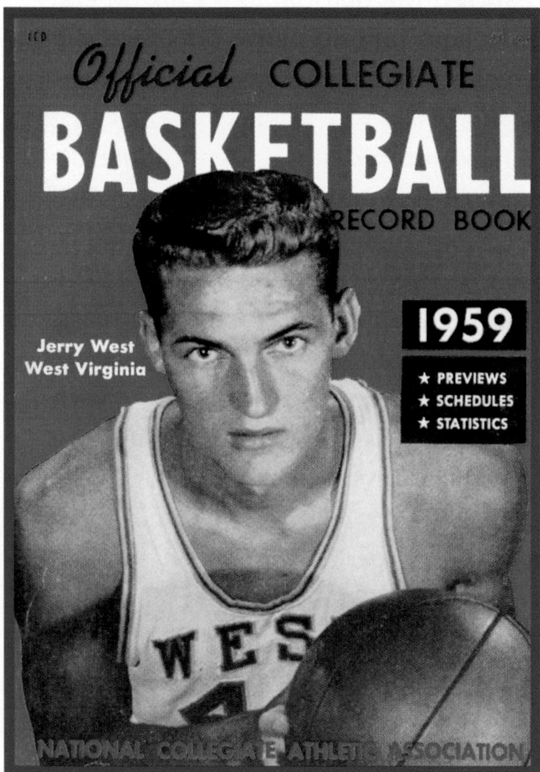

Twice an All-American at West Virginia, Jerry West continued his storybook basketball career with the Los Angeles Lakers of the NBA. West is considered perhaps the deadliest shooter ever to play the game.

As great as these players were, however, they ended up taking a back seat to the two men who dominated college basketball during the 1950s: Bill Russell and Wilt Chamberlain. Russell played for the University of San Francisco, which had won the NIT championship in 1949 with an all-white squad. In 1951, coach Phil Woolpert decided to tap into the Bay Area's black basketball talent and came up with a defensive genius named K.C. Jones. In 1952, he brought Russell over from Oakland, and by 1955 there were a half-dozen black players on the Dons. Russell was not much of a shooter, but he was a great rebounder and passer, and a revolutionary defender. In an era when most centers could barely get off the floor, Russell had a better vertical leap than most modern players. He also had long, long arms, and perhaps the greatest shot-blocking timing in the game's history. As a result, no one could shoot against him. He completely shut down the lane, and took the opposing center out of almost every game he played. Russell could also run the floor, and many of his points came at the end of a fast break with his man huffing and puffing around mid-court while he stuffed the ball. During his college career, Russell typically got 20 points and 20 rebounds a game, and it was not unusual for him to

Bill Russell soars toward the hoop for the University of San Francisco in 1956. Russell's greatest talents lay in rebounding, defense, shot-blocking, and leadership—he drove his USF teams to two national championships and an incredible 55 straight victories.

block a dozen shots. He led the Dons to back-to-back NCAA championships in 1955 and 1956, and pushed them to a legendary winning streak that ultimately reached 55 games.

Chamberlain, who came to the University of Kansas in 1955, was something that had been unimaginable just a few years earlier: a seven-footer with perfect coordination and immense athletic ability. An unstoppable basketball player, he was also a world-class track and field athlete who could sprint, high jump, and shot-put. So terrified of Chamberlain were the country's college coaches that they instituted a number of rules changes, including the widening of the lane and a ban on offensive goaltending. They also put in a rule stating that a player could not jump from the foul line and dunk his free throws—a Chamberlain specialty in high school. In the days when most college teams did not have coordinated player over 6'5", Chamberlain was a coach's worst nightmare.

The only defense against Chamberlain was to keep him from getting the ball, and this was accomplished in two ways. First, opposing teams simply waited as long as they could before taking a shot. Second, they often put four men on Chamberlain, daring his fellow Jayhawks to attempt wide-open jumpers from short range. Chamberlain still topped 30 points and 20 rebounds most of the time, while his teammates shot well enough to win the majority of their games. In the 1957 NCAA final, the University of North Carolina played a perfect game against Chamberlain, and the other Jayhawks went cold. It still took two overtimes, but the Tar Heels pulled out a 54-53

Wilt ("The Stilt") Chamberlain was a national cover story even in high school. Standing 7'1", with great strength, speed, jumping ability, and coordination, he was the most dominant player in college basketball from the minute he arrived at Kansas University.

victory. The stalling and mobbing tactics continued the following year, and Chamberlain said enough is enough—he was not having fun, and he was not making money. He left Kansas prior to his senior season to tour with the Harlem Globetrotters for a year, and then entered the NBA as soon as he became eligible.

The NBA Finds Its Legs

On August 3, 1949, the NBL and BAA joined forces and the National Basketball Association was born. It was a big baby—17 teams in three divisions for its first season, with a total of 12 teams qualifying for the playoffs. The Minneapolis Lakers won the first NBA championship, which was their third league title in a row, albeit in three different leagues. George Mikan and Jim Pollard were joined by forward Vern Mikkelsen and guard Slater Martin, who quickly established themselves as two of the best players in pro ball. Double-teaming Mikan was no longer the key to beating Minneapolis, for there were now several players who could score consistently. Free to muscle his way to the basket, and at the height of his powers, Mikan regularly scored 25 to 30 points a game and even topped 50 in one contest.

Right behind the Lakers in terms of personnel were the Rochester Royals, the other great team of the NBA's formative years. Unlike Minneapolis, the Royals concentrated on moving the ball quickly and finding the open man—an approach that became more effective as the season wore on and players tended to lose a half-step. Guard Bob Davies led a veteran squad that included backcourt mates Bobby Wanzer and Red Holzman, as well as big men Arnie Risen and Jack Coleman. Davies, the NBL's MVP in 1947, continued his spectacular playmaking in the NBA, making the all-league squad four times in a row and distributing the ball so well that only a couple of points separated the per-game scoring averages of his fellow starters. The Royals won 15 straight games to tie the Lakers for the NBA's Central Division crown in 1949–50, but lost to Mikan and his cohorts in the playoffs. In 1950–51, the Royals returned the favor, dumping Minneapolis in the semis to reach the NBA finals, where they beat the New York Knicks.

By the 1951–52 season the NBA had shaken off its smaller franchises and become a solid 10-team circuit. Revelations of college betting scandals had convinced many college "purists" to give the NBA a chance. With the amateurs now considered "dirty," the pros did not look so bad, and interest in the NBA began to build—especially after commissioner Maurice Podoloff banned accused fixers Alex Groza and Ralph Beard for their alleged point-shaving activities back at the University of Kentucky. Podoloff also spearheaded a rules change that saw the foul lane widened from 6 to 12 feet. This change was to keep big guys (specifically George Mikan) from setting up a couple of feet from the basket and simply elbowing their way to an easy layup or baby hook. Mikan got the ball less and missed more of his shots, but he was still the top player in the league. The top scorer, however, was 23-year-old Paul Arizin of the Philadelphia Warriors, who hit for 25.4 points per game from his forward slot. An asthma sufferer who sometimes seemed on the verge of collapse, his springy legs and quick release enabled him to score from anywhere on the court. With veteran teammates Joe Fulks and Andy Phillip around to show him the ropes, the 6'4" Arizin became the model for the "small forwards" of the 1950s.

Beyond the individual achievements of its best players, the NBA rewarded its newfound fans with a fantastic season in 1951–52. The league had been pared down to two divisions, and each featured tight, multiteam races. Better still, the Knicks surprised the Celtics and Nats in the playoffs to reach the finals again, spurring great enthusiasm in the very city where the college fixing scandals had originated. Unfortunately, New York lost again in seven games, this time to the Lakers. The outcome might have been very different had the New Yorkers not run into some bad luck. In Game 1, the referees whistled the Lakers for a shooting foul but somehow did not see Al McGuire's shot go in. The game went into overtime, and the Knicks lost. After winning Game 2, the Knicks lost Games 3 and 4, which were played in an armory (instead of Madison Square Garden) because the circus was in town. Losing home-court advantage to a bunch of clowns and elephants probably cost New York the championship. That the circus was considered more important than the NBA Finals shows just how far the league had to go before achieving major-league status.

The strength of its New York franchise, however, was a huge plus. Although little is remembered about the Knicks of the early 1950s, they ranked as one of the last great old-style basketball teams. Coach Joe Lapchick updated the quick passing, tight defense, and heads-up teamwork of the Original Celtics and collected a group of players who were talented and experienced enough to blend together and adjust to the changing forces in the game. At guard, Lapchick had Al McGuire's playmaking brother, Dick. He and outside shooting specialists Max Zaslofsky and Carl Braun kept defenses honest at the perimeter, while centers Connie Simmons and Sweetwater Clifton—the premier black player in the league during the early 1950s—took care of business around the boards. On the wings were Vince Boryla, Ernie Vandeweghe, and Harry "The Horse" Gallatin, whose superb timing made him the league's best-rebounding forward. The Knicks

MR. BASKETBALL

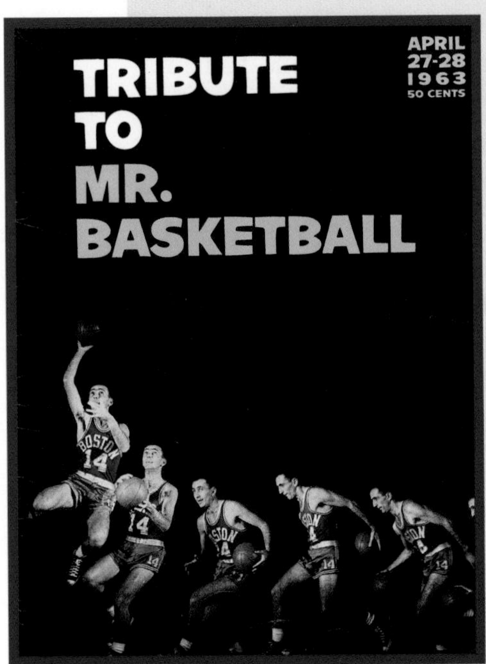

Bob Cousy's magic with the basketball baffled defenders and kept fans on the edge of their seats.

In the years following World War II, no player did more to popularize basketball than Bob Cousy. At Holy Cross, he perfected the behind-the-back dribble Marques Haynes and Bob Davies had popularized, and was a favorite of crowds wherever he played. Cousy's entry into the NBA, however, was anything but smooth. The league had just consolidated, and players were being redistributed left and right. Cousy was drafted by the Tri-Cities Blackhawks (the forerunner of today's Atlanta Hawks), but then dealt to the Chicago Stags for veteran guard Frank Brian during the summer. Shortly thereafter, the Chicago franchise folded, so Cousy's name was literally dropped into a hat with the names of the other Stag guards, Max Zaslofsky and Andy Phillip. The Celtics watched as the Knicks got Zaslofsky and the Warriors got Phillip, leaving Boston coach Red Auerbach wondering why nothing ever seemed to go his way. Auerbach did not see how Cousy would make it as a pro. He ran too much for the plodding pro game, and his fancy passes were just as likely to break a teammate's nose as lead to a basket.

As things turned out, Cousy was by far the best of three Stag backcourt men, and even better in the pros than he had been in college. With their young star dribbling and passing up a storm, the Celtics ran the fast

reached the finals for a third straight time in 1952–53, but lost to the Lakers again.

The 1953–54 season played out as expected, with the Minneapolis Lakers and Knicks winning their respective divisions. The Syracuse Nationals sprung a surprise in the postseason by sweeping both the Knicks and Celtics out of the playoffs to earn a showdown with the Lakers in the finals. An exciting seesaw battle produced three victories for each team, but Game 7 belonged to George Mikan. Mikan, though still a couple of months short of his 30th birthday, called it quits to become the general manager of the Lakers and open a law practice in Minneapolis. He left the NBA as the regular-season and career record holder in points scored and points per game.

The Shot Clock

Pro basketball entered its modern age during the 1954–55 season, when the NBA decided to add the 24-second shot clock to its games.

break when it was there, and worked a methodical half-court offense when it was not. Either way, Cousy's magicianlike ballhandling abilities made the Celtics a winning team. His ability to bring the ball through his legs or behind his back on the dead run meant that defenders could not block his progress on the fast break. And once the other Celtics got used to his passes, the team's offense really began to click.

Cousy could hit a man with a pass without even glancing in his direction, and this had a big effect on the way defense was played in the NBA. Prior to Cousy's arrival, a typical pro defender played off his man by five to ten feet until he got the ball. The methodical two-handed chest passes most ballplayers used were easy to read, and there was plenty of time to tighten up on defense when a player got the ball. By contrast, Cousy could fire a pass to a teammate without tipping off the defense, meaning Celtic shooters were receiving the ball with that five-to-ten-foot buffer still intact. When defenders caught on to Cousy and began guarding more closely, the Boston players would wait for the right moment then break toward the basket to receive a Cousy pass. It took a couple of years for this kind of teamwork to develop, but once it did the Celtics became a very special team.

Not surprisingly, Cousy led the league in assists for eight consecutive seasons. He could also shoot the ball, both from the outside and in heavy traffic, and he was perfectly built for basketball. Although Cousy stood 6'1" (average at the time for an NBA guard), he was a big man with large hands, sloping shoulders, long arms, and strong legs. He also possessed extraordinary peripheral vision. Ultimately, though, it was Cousy's mind that separated him from the rest. He knew when to play it safe, when to take chances, and when to have fun and improvise. By the time the Celtics started surrounding him with good players, he was the top star in the NBA. And to the enormous delight of the once-skeptical Auerbach, Cousy proved that he had what it took to make a good team great.

Prior to this change games had slowed to a crawl in the closing minutes—the team in the lead would freeze the ball, and the team trying to catch up would start fouling to get it back. In other words, the excitement often ended just when it should have reached its crescendo. This worried NBA owners, who at first ordered referees to assess technical fouls to teams that tried to run minutes at a time off the clock. When this did not work, they took decisive action.

The shot clock, it was hoped, would curtail these practices and spur a little more action at other times. It is hard to believe that the man who came up with this idea—Syracuse owner Danny Biasone—envisioned the enormous impact this innovation would have.

The shot clock changed everything. Teams no longer sauntered down the court after the ball changed hands; they ran. Players who could create their own shots flourished, while those who needed a lot of ball movement to get open fell by the wayside. Stamina became a major issue, and a lot of the league's big, slow players became instant part-timers. Players who could catch the ball and shoot it quickly became highly prized. So did good offensive rebounders, as teams attempted, made, and missed more shots than ever before.

How dramatic was the difference? The lowest-scoring team in the NBA in 1954–55 (the Hawks) averaged 87 points a game—the same as the 1953–54 scoring champs (the Celtics) had. And overall, scoring rose a whopping 27 points a game. Yet it is interesting to note that the actual makeup of a typical team was not altered all that much. Scoring went up across the board—on average, everyone from the league's Top 10 scorers down to a given team's sixth and seventh men scored an extra basket a game.

As players got more comfortable working with the clock, scoring continued to climb. By the end of the 1950s it was not unusual for teams to combine for 220 to 250 points a contest. Commissioner Maurice Podoloff observed that the NBA might not have lasted had it not been for Biasone's idea. It certainly would not have gotten a national television contract. No one would have stayed tuned to games where teams were content to dribble out the clock.

Along with the 24-second clock came a rule limiting teams to six fouls per quarter. In the days when a nonshooting foul resulted in one free throw, this was important, for after the sixth foul a player got to take two shots from the line. This meant there was little to gain by constant fouling. A team could stop the clock and get the ball back, but ran the risk of giving an opponent two free points.

The players benefiting most from the NBA's new look were forwards who could hit the medium-range shot and also slash to the basket. George Yardley (who perfected the double-pump), Schayes, and Pettit saw their scoring and rebounding averages soar. They could finish fast breaks, get good shots from 10 to 15 feet, and outjump the league's lumbering big men when the ball came off the glass. There were no mobile centers at this time—the men who played this position were typically big, strong, and scored on tip-ins and hook shots. When the ball went the other way, they normally trailed the play. Anyone could see, however, that a quick, coordinated center would eat the old guys alive. And in the mid-1950s there were several in the college

Long, lean Bob Pettit could either slash to the basket or pull up for the jump shot, and was one of the highest-scoring forwards of the 1950s and early 1960s. Here he glides in for a layup.

ranks who would almost instantly transform the game.

The first to hit the league was Bill Russell, from the University of San Francisco. Red Auerbach, who had been coaching the Celtics since 1950, had built a team based on the fast-break. He had the passers, shooters, and ball handlers required to make this approach work, but needed someone who could dominate the defensive boards and then hustle down the court ahead of the opposition's center. Auerbach watched Russell become this player in college, and plotted to get him in the 1956 draft. The Rochester Royals and St. Louis Hawks picked ahead of the Celtics, but Auerbach knew that the cash-poor Royals had no chance of signing Russell, who was being offered a huge salary by the Harlem Globetrotters. The Hawks were another story. Auerbach was terrified by the idea of Bob Pettit and Bill Russell on the same front line, so he made the team an offer it could not refuse. The Boston coach dangled veteran center Ed Macauley—a big college star with St. Louis University—and rookie forward Cliff Hagan, a big scorer for the University of Kentucky who had grown into a monster during two years in the military. Auerbach knew he was handing the Hawks the Western Division title, but he felt Russell would turn his team into a dynasty. Auerbach was correct on both points. The Hawks dominated the West for years, while the Boston Celtics became the most balanced team in the NBA.

The Rise of the Celtics

Once the Boston Celtics obtained Bill Russell, they could put a player at each position who knew his role and played it perfectly. If a player had a weakness, Auerbach made sure he was not on the floor unless his teammates were able to pick up the slack. And because the Celtics acquired so many players who fit into this system, they were always well-rested enough to run an opponent out of the building if they got the chance.

The veterans on the Celtic teams of the 1950s were guards Bob Cousy and Bill Sharman. Cousy, of course, ran the offense. On the break, he would take the outlet pass from Russell and charge up the court. If Cousy saw a teammate out ahead of the pack he would rifle a pass to him for an easy layup. If not, he would swerve to the middle and stop at the top of the key, where he would either shoot, leave the ball for a trailing man, or thread a pass to someone cutting in from the side. When the ball came up the court at a slower pace, Cousy often drew a double team, which left Sharman with room to shoot. And what a shot he was—easily the best of his generation. A conditioning freak who was always the fittest man on the court, Sharman was as deadly in the last minute of play as he was in the first, and if teams tried to foul him they were really asking for trouble, for he also happened to be the top free-throw shooter in the league.

At the forward positions in the 1950s were young guns Tom Heinsohn, Jim Loscutoff, Frank Ramsey, and Sam Jones. Heinsohn loved to shoot so much that he was nicknamed "Ack-Ack" after the sound a rapid-firing antiaircraft gun made. He was a tough, aggressive player whose shot went in like a line drive, and although he was paid to put points on the board he was a fierce rebounder, too. Loscutoff's primary job was to snag rebounds. He usually played about half the game, depending upon how well Boston was controlling the boards.

When Auerbach needed a little more finesse he sent in his special "sixth man," Ramsey. The 6'3" Kentucky grad had played guard in college for Adolph Rupp, but the Celtics liked to use him as a small forward, where he could use his quickness and understanding of the game to exploit opposing forwards. Ice water flowed through Ramsey's veins, and it was he who was often called upon to take the team's most important shots. In fact, it was his 20-footer in double-overtime that won Game 7 for Boston in the 1957 NBA Finals and gave Boston its first of many NBA titles.

Jones, who turned down a scholarship from Notre Dame to attend a smaller school closer to home, was selected in the first round by Auerbach in 1957. Everyone thought the coach had lost his mind, but when the rangy forward unveiled his blinding speed and unorthodox bankshot, they knew Auerbach had done his homework. Jones would come off the bench as a swingman for several season before earning the starting guard spot when Sharman began to slow down. Also on Auerbach's bench in the 1950s were Andy Phillip and Arnie Risen, who were too old to play more than a few minutes a game, but who could be devastatingly effective in short spurts.

This collection of players would have been good enough to challenge for the NBA title all by itself. The addition of Russell, however, made everyone better. Never before had a center played with such ferocity and sheer athletic ability. A student of the center position, Russell was a phenomenal shot-blocker and intimidator, effectively closing down the lane on defense. Because the vast majority of NBA players were still operating "below the rim," Russell could cover an enormous area with his long arms, great lateral mobility, and jumping prowess. He also boxed out better than anyone in history, which helped him average more than 20 rebounds a game.

Russell was the key to the Celtic fast break. He could grab a ball off the glass and fire it out to a guard in one smooth motion, meaning Celtic opponents had to start thinking about getting back on defense while they were still on offense. Russell's dominance near the basket enabled a Boston guard to release from his man when a shot went up, putting him several steps ahead on the fast break. If Russell saw this and was able to collect the rebound, he would fire the ball the length of the court. The thing that just killed opponents, though, was that Russell was fast enough to function as the finisher on the fast break, or follow up a teammate's miss with an offensive rebound and dunk—even when he started the play at the other end.

When Russell joined the Celtics in December of 1956 (after taking time out to win a gold medal at the Olympics in Australia) the team came together almost immediately. Boston won the Eastern Division easily and won its first championship in a seven-game thriller against the Hawks. In 1957–58, St. Louis and Boston met in the finals again. The Russell trade had indeed helped the Hawks, as Hagan and Macauley combined with Jack Coleman and Bob Pettit to give the Hawks the league's strongest frontcourt. They benefited further by the fine play of guards Jack McMahon and ex-Laker Slater Martin. This pair concentrated on feeding the ball inside, and saved their energy to play harassing defense against opposing guards. In Game 3, with the series tied at

1–1, Russell badly sprained his ankle and had to sit out for three games. The Celtics lost two of those games, and Auerbach reluctantly inserted Russell into Game 6. Sadly, he could not jump or move quickly, and Hawk superstar Pettit took full advantage of this weakness, shredding Boston's interior defense for 50 points. Even without Russell, who played just 20 minutes, the Celtics nearly held on to force a Game 7, losing 110-109. It would be another nine years before the guys in green walked off the court as losers again.

Going Above the Rim

Russell's success in college and the pros opened the eyes of fans, coaches, and owners to the kind of basketball the future might hold. Although most big-time players were white, it became increasingly obvious that the faster, more vertical brand of basketball first pioneered by the all-black Renaissance teams of the 1930s and 1940s would soon be the rule in the NBA instead of the exception. Black players had long played the game "differently" than whites. Now they finally were gaining recognition for playing it as well or better. This opened the NBA doors to a group of wonderful players, and by the beginning of the 1960s these black stars had played a major role in bringing basketball very close to its present form.

The Syracuse Nationals drafted two of the best shooting guards in basketball in Hal Greer and Dick Barnett. Forwards Willie Naulls and Johnny Green joined the Knicks out of college and became two of the best rebounding forwards. Al Attles of the Philadelphia Warriors and Lenny Wilkens of the Hawks smashed the lingering stereotype of black athletes as more "instinctive" than smart by gaining wide recognition as two of the most intelligent players in the league. The Royals, after moving from Rochester to Cincinnati in 1957, lost one of the NBA's most promising black players when forward Maurice Stokes was struck down by encephalitis. Like Russell, Stokes could get off the ground and get down the court, and for a while—when hot-shooting Jack Twyman teamed with Stokes in the frontcourt—it looked as if the stumbling Royals might make some noise in the NBAs Western Division. Indeed, it is interesting to imagine what might have been, for following this tragedy the Royals drafted three more excellent black players: center Wayne Embry, forward Bob Boozer, and Oscar Robertson.

Robertson was every defensive player's nightmare. He could knock down 20-footers if left open, or work the ball in close and then hit a runner or a fall-away jumper. He also could put a couple of moves on his man and drive to the hoop. At 6'5", the "Big O" was a handful, and an all-around basketball genius like the game had never seen. He was a smart and aggressive passer who was quite willing to zip the ball to a teammate when he found himself double-teamed. And if that teammate put the ball up, Robertson could go to the glass stronger than any guard who ever played. Today the "triple-double," the statistical feat of notching 10 or more points, rebounds, and assists in a single game, is the measure of all-around greatness; players like Magic Johnson or Grant Hill might accomplish this in a handful of games each season. But the Big O *averaged* a triple-double in 1961–62, dishing out 11.4 assists, plucking 12.5 rebounds, and dropping in a whopping 30.8 points per game. He stayed close to this level throughout the prime of his career.

Though not quite the all-around player Robertson was, Elgin Baylor of the Lakers was more spectacular. He would slice in from the wing and go right to the basket, making last-second adjustments in the air so he could flick the ball into the basket. If the opportunity presented itself, he would throw down a monstrous jam—this many years before it became the NBA's signature play. He electrified the fans like no one had before; they knew that on any given night he could score 40, 50, or even 60 points—in a 1960 game against the Knicks, he scored 71. Almost no video footage exists from his first few years with the Lakers, but by all accounts he was the Michael Jordan of his day. And like Jordan, he was not a one-dimensional player—Baylor passed and rebounded as well as any forward in the league.

Elgin Baylor of the Lakers was the Michael Jordan of his day, a player whose extraordinary leaping ability—his hang time—enabled him to float over defenders, make mid-air adjustments, then flip the ball into the hoop.

Of the group of black players that came into the NBA during this period, no one had a bigger effect on the league itself than Wilt Chamberlain. He towered over everyone, and he had a fully developed set of offensive skills that no one knew how to stop. In college, his statistics were impressive, but they barely hinted at what was to come. Chamberlain's Jayhawks played without a shot clock. In the NBA, the ball went up three or four times a minute. Though few doubted Chamberlain would dominate in the pros, could anyone have predicted how thoroughly? Apparently not, for the harder teams worked to defend Chamberlain, the more he scored. The more aggressive they were at keeping him off the boards, the more rebounds he grabbed. And no matter how many drivers they sent down the lane, or how many balls they threw into the post, they could never foul Chamberlain out of a game.

Known as "Wilt the Stilt" and the "Big Dipper," Chamberlain joined the Philadelphia Warriors for the 1959–60 season and had shattered virtually every NBA scoring record by the end of his rookie year. Free from the triple- and quadruple-teaming he faced in college, Chamberlain shot around 30 times a game and made about half of his shots. Unfortunately, he could only hit about half of his free throws, so his scoring average remained at mere mortal levels, at least for his first two seasons. Then, in 1961–62, he decided to take around 40 shots a game. The result was a scoring average that seems like a misprint: 50.4 points a game. During that season, against the New York Knicks, Chamberlain even scored 100 points in a game.

Contrary to popular belief, Chamberlain actually had a talented supporting cast during the early 1960s. He was only a "one-man team" when he wanted to be. The Warriors still had Paul Arizin, who was good for 20 points a game, while Tom Meschery played the enforcer's role at the other forward. Feeding Wilt the ball were Guy Rodgers, one of the great assist men in NBA history, and veteran Tom Gola, who at 6'6" was the league's first big guard. This group was good for 45 to 50 wins a year, and finished a strong second to the Celtics during Chamberlain's first three seasons.

It was Chamberlain's battles with Bill Russell that captured the imagination of America's sports fans and earned for the NBA what it most desperately needed: a national television contract. The league's schedule-makers made sure that these two giants met on Sundays as often as possible, for that was the day that NBC (and later ABC) aired its weekly national game. To watch these two men battle each other was almost surrealistic at times, for they were so clearly playing at a level to which no one else on the court could aspire. Even viewers who did not fully understand what they were watching got the sense that every time Russ and Wilt took the court, history was being rewritten. Each made the other better, and ultimately more important. So many fans got turned onto NBA basketball by this pair that they soon took on mythic proportions. Russell was cast as the hard-working underdog who would gladly take one for the team, while Chamberlain represented the heartless giant who destroyed everything he touched, including his own team. The quality of play was rising by the year in the NBA, but at the time these two figures were so dominant that hardly anyone noticed.

The Changing College Game

College basketball during the 1960s was a continuation of the trends established during the 1950s. A series of immensely talented individual players captured the public's imagination with their offensive and defensive feats, while the offensive and defensive systems created by the game's top coaches became more and more sophisticated. This was wonderful for the fans, because on any given night they might see two great stars go against each other, a great star up against a great system, or two great systems meeting in a clash of theories and ideologies. And thanks to a new generation of coaches and an influx of players from the nation's inner cities, the level and style of play climbed steadily throughout the 1960s.

In the early part of the decade, Jerry Lucas of Ohio State University was the most recognizable player in college ball. A nationally known star in high school and a straight-A student, he joined the Buckeyes on an academic scholarship and averaged more than 26 points and 16 rebounds during his first varsity campaign in 1959–60. By season's end, the 6'7" sophomore had led the team through the NCAA tournament in record form, as they beat each of their opponents by 15 points or more on their way to the national title. Lucas was joined on the Buckeyes by John Havlicek, and they teamed together over the next two years to form the nucleus of one of basketball's

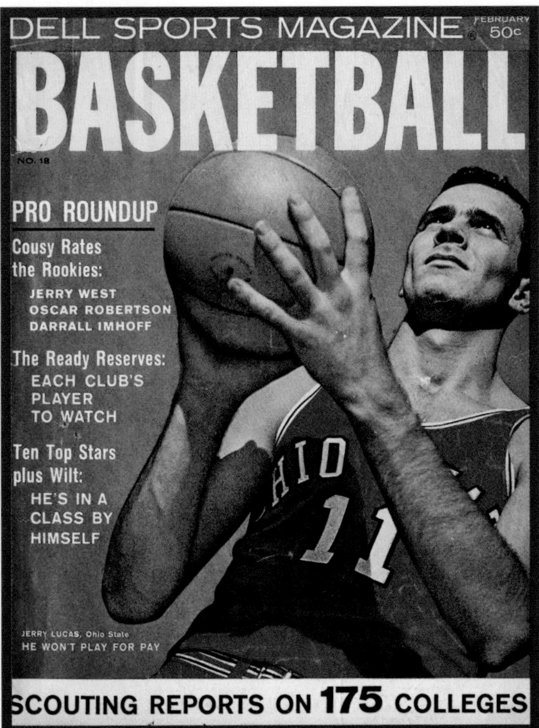

The perfect image of the scholar-athlete, Jerry Lucas led Ohio State to three straight trips to the NCAA final in the early 1960s.

greatest college teams. From 1959–60 to 1961–62, Ohio State went 78–6 and reached the NCAA final each year. Lucas appeared on the covers of countless magazines and earned two Player of the Year trophies.

The team that unseated Ohio State and its two stars in the 1961 and 1962 NCAA finals was, predictably, a team that had no stars at all: the University of Cincinnati Bearcats, who had failed to win a title when they had Oscar Robertson. After the Big O graduated, coach George Smith handed over the team's reins to assistant Ed Jucker, who molded a group led by center Paul Hogue and forward Tom Thacker into an unselfish and cohesive unit. Jucker convinced them to replace the old give-the-ball-to-Oscar offense with a tight pattern offense designed to create easy buckets. It was the same offensive concept that had knocked the Bearcats out of the 1959 and 1960 NCAA tournaments, when Pete Newell's University of California team back-doored the Bearcats to death. Jucker also taught his team a man-to-zone defense inspired by Hank Iba, which had defensive players away from the ball dropping off their men and into a zone, where they could shut down the passing lanes and help with double teams. The result was a 27–3 record in 1960–61 and 29–2 in 1961–62, and amazing back-to-back NCAA titles. In 1962–63, the Bearcats again made it to the NCAA final, but were beaten by Loyola University in overtime. Loyola, like Cincinnati the year before, played the final with four black starters.

This was viewed as something of a milestone in basketball until 1966, when Texas Western University started five black players in the NCAA final and beat lily-white Kentucky. Coach Don Haskins had imported a group of street-smart inner-city players to the sleepy town of El Paso, and they produced a 23–1 mark in 1965–66. The Miners ranged in size from 5'10" to 6'7", and each player could handle the ball and play suffocating man-to-man defense for 40 minutes. If a team tried to run against the Miners, they would outrun them. If they tried to rough them up, they would out-slug them. And if a game turned into a shooting contest, then coach Haskins knew he had a victory all but assured, because no one could put the ball up against his team's defensive onslaught and expect to make more than a third of their shots. In the landmark final against Kentucky, they controlled the game from beginning to end and showed in-

David ("Big Daddy") Lattin of Texas Western reaches around to block a Kentucky layup attempt early in the 1966 NCAA final. The all-black Texas Western squad beat lily-white Kentucky, sending ripples throughout the college-basketball world. No major program would ever again engage in white-only recruiting.

credible poise on the foul line, where the game was ultimately won. The importance of this championship was that it broke the college color line once and for all. Beginning that spring, no major program engaged in white-only recruiting ever again.

The Celtics Dynasty

The 1960s may have been a time of great upheaval in most quarters of society, but not in the NBA. Somehow or other, Red Auerbach and his gang were going to raise another championship banner to the Boston Garden rafters each spring, and everyone else in the league seemed resigned to this fact. The Celtics grew older in the early 1960s, but Auerbach continued to find players who fit perfectly into his system. It was very frustrating for Boston's opponents. The first Celtic star to hang up his sneakers was Bill Sharman, who retired after the team's five-game victory over the Hawks in the 1961 NBA Finals. He was replaced by Sam Jones, who went on to lead the team in scoring for the next six seasons. Bob Cousy called it quits after the Celtics trounced the Lakers in the 1963 finals. He was replaced by Russell's college teammate K.C. Jones, who became the team's point man and played defense even harder than Cousy had. Jim Loscutoff was replaced by Satch Sanders, who played the same role of rebounder and far surpassed Loscutoff on defense. When Frank Ramsey could no longer come off the bench with the same old zip, swingman John Havlicek filled his shoes and gave Boston the same combination of quickness and smarts that the "Kentucky Colonel" had. Tom Heinsohn continued to do everything well, and Auerbach managed to pick up quality veterans for his bench, including Clyde Lovellette, Carl Braun, and Willie Naulls. Beginning with their 1959 championship, the Celtics won the

As his Celtics put the finishing touches on the 1965 NBA title—the team's seventh-straight championship—coach Red Auerbach smiles a Cheshire-cat grin and puffs on his customary victory cigar.

NBA title a mind-boggling eight straight times. They beat the Hawks in 1960 and 1961, the Warriors in 1964, and the Lakers the other five times.

When the Hawks began to stumble in the early part of the decade, a power vacuum developed in the NBA's Western Division, and thanks to Elgin Baylor and Jerry West, the Lakers (who transferred to Los Angeles in 1960) filled it. Baylor continued to play wondrous basketball until he broke his kneecap in 1965, and was still great after his rehab and return. West broke into the league in 1960 and turned into one of the best two-way guards the sport has ever seen. His focus and concentration were legendary, and he was absolutely fearless when it came to taking control of a game. Considered by many to be the greatest clutch shooter in NBA history, West was also something exceptionally rare: a shot-blocking guard. And he was everything else you wanted a guard to be—tall, quick, agile, instinctive, and selfish only when he needed to be.

The Lakers had what it took to win their division, but could never match up properly with the Celtics. Baylor and West were unquestionably the best forward and guard on the court when Boston and L.A. met. But beyond these two the Lakers lacked championship-caliber players, and their bench was a wasteland compared to what the Celtics had. Dick Barnett complimented West fairly well in the backcourt, and Rudy LaRusso held his own as a power forward, but the Lakers never found an answer to Bill Russell, and he absolutely murdered them.

Wilt Breaks Through

The 1966–67 season finally saw the Celtics' string broken. Wilt Chamberlain had moved from Philadelphia to San Francisco with the Warriors in 1963, but after reaching the finals in 1964 the team began to disintegrate. The morning after the 1965 NBA All-Star Game, the basketball world was shocked to hear that Chamberlain had been traded. He was returning home to Philadelphia, where the Syracuse Nationals had set up shop and renamed themselves the 76ers.

Chamberlain could not have been more delighted. He was joining a franchise that had developed a reputation for playing team basketball. Perhaps, Chamberlain thought, they would have a shot at overtaking the Celtics. And they would—under the coaching of Dolph Schayes, the team went 55–25 and edged Boston for the Eastern Division title in 1965. But once again, Russ got the best of Wilt in the playoffs, as the Celtics blew out the 76ers 4–1 in the semifinals.

Chamberlain was beside himself. What more did he have to do?

The answer was that Wilt had to do less. Try as he might, Chamberlain could not personally outscore an opponent. Auerbach knew this and the Celtics had always beaten Chamberlain's teams by neutralizing his teammates and then forcing him to win games all by himself. Occasionally, he did. But in a playoff series against a quality team, this strategy just would not work.

Alex Hannum, who had coached Chamberlain in San Francisco, realized this early on. In fact, before the big trade he had come close to convincing Wilt that his greatest potential was not as a scorer, but as someone who had the ability to dominate every other facet of play. The 76ers dumped Schayes and hired Hannum for the 1966–67 campaign.

The 76ers were indeed a talented club. Flanking Chamberlain on the forward line were veteran Chet Walker and second-year star Billy Cunningham, each of whom was an excellent shooter and rebounder. Luke Jackson, a tough, aggressive inside player, could either play beside Chamberlain or give him an occasional breather at center. Hal Greer and Wally Jones were the guards, with Greer a proven 20-point scorer and Jones an excellent ball handler. Veteran Larry Costello, a rock-solid defender, was also available for backcourt duty. Coach Hannum convinced Chamberlain that if he concentrated on rebounding, shot-blocking, setting picks, and passing out of the double teams he would face, the team was capable of scoring 120 points a game. The 76ers had the talent to fast-break or play a conservative half-court offense—either way, Wilt would still be the key man. Chamberlain agreed to give the plan a try.

The 76ers began winning almost every game they played. As the victories piled up, Chamberlain embraced his new role with great relish. He limited his shooting to dunks, finger rolls, and tip-ins and shot an incredible 68.3 percent for the season. He led the league with 24 rebounds a game and finished third in assists with nearly 8 per contest—more than playmaking guards Jerry West and Lenny Wilkens. Chamberlain's scoring dropped to 24.1 points per game, but his 76er teammates added a whopping 100 points per game on top of that. Philadelphia finished the year at

Before the 1966–67 season, Philadelphia 76ers coach Alex Hannum convinced Wilt Chamberlain to involve his teammates in the offense rather than trying to score himself every time he got the ball. The result was a record-breaking 68–13 year for the Sixers—and, at last, a taste of championship champagne for the Big Dipper.

68–13, which was by far the best mark in history to that time.

The Celtics, who picked up high-scoring forward Bailey Howell in a slick off-season deal, also improved themselves. And in an interesting move, Red Auerbach turned over the team's coaching reins to Bill Russell, making him the first black coach in a major American sports league. As always, Russell managed to handle Chamberlain's rebounding and scoring, but he had no way to control Wilt's newfound passing prowess. When the playoffs rolled around, the younger, bigger, faster 76ers just rolled over the Celtics, beating them 4–1.

In the finals, Philly faced the surprising San Francisco Warriors, who had recovered from the Chamberlain trade to assemble a fine team. Young Nate Thurmond—a power forward when he played beside Chamberlain—had grown into the center's role nicely, and was the only man in the league besides Russell who could give Wilt a decent game. Second-year forward Rick Barry provided great shooting and excellent passing from the perimeter, while Chamberlain's former teammates, Al Attles and Tom Meschery, played important defensive roles. Ex-Celtic Bill Sharman was hired to coach the Warriors after Hannum left for Philadelphia. He whipped these players into Sharman-like shape and taught them the quick-strike offense that he had helped perfect in Boston. The Warriors played the 76ers close, but in the end they too were overpowered. When the season was done, Chamberlain was being hailed as a new man, the 76ers were being called the best team ever, and the Celtics were being eulogized like a dear, departed uncle. On the first two points, the experts were correct. On the last, they had greatly underestimated Mr. Russell.

Making Room: New Teams and a New League

For the first time since its creation, the National Basketball Association was truly ready to expand. The game had finally developed a legitimate coast-to-coast fan base, and pro rosters were loaded with talented young players. Following the 1967 NBA Finals, an expansion draft was held to stock

Scoring machine Rick Barry—here bending into his deadly accurate underhand free-throw motion—was supposed to have been the poster boy for the infant ABA. Legal wrangling and injuries, however, limited his contributions, and he eventually returned to the NBA and led the Golden State Warriors to a championship.

two new teams, the San Diego Rockets and Seattle Supersonics. The league encouraged its new entries to stick with talent plucked from NBA rosters, and steer clear of the hundreds of ex-college players who were performing for industrial, semipro, and minor-league teams.

These players had long made up basketball's "underworld." Some of them were quite good at one or two things, but had never rounded out their games. Others had been the victims of bad luck, bad timing, bad press, or bad reputations. Most had taken a shot at the NBA at some point but had fallen short. A few had probably been good enough, but had been cut because of racial quotas. Many believe that, for most of the 1960s, there was an unwritten, unspoken rule in the NBA that you did not play five black men at the same time. This untapped pool of raw talent would ultimately get its chance to shine in the American Basketball Association.

The ABA was dreamed up by Dennis Murphy, who was part sports-marketing genius and part huckster. He was convinced there was enough interest, enough money, and enough decent players to put together a second pro league, so he set about the task of lining up investors. When the league's inaugural season began 11 franchises took the court, with teams in Minneapolis, Pittsburgh, Indianapolis, Louisville, New Orleans, Houston, Dallas, Denver, Anaheim, Oakland, and Teaneck. Each was a large city that had displayed an appetite for pro sports, with the exception of Teaneck, a small town located in densely populated northern New Jersey. The ABA had talked George Mikan into becoming its commissioner, and he worked with the owners to give the league a distinctive look, including a red-white-and-blue basketball and a three-point line, which was set 25 feet away from the basket. The shot clock was set at 30 seconds to give teams six extra ticks to work the ball into shooting range.

To steal some thunder away from the NBA, the ABA went after the established league's first-round draft choices and a couple of its young stars. Rick Barry, the reigning NBA scoring champ, signed to play with the Oakland Oaks, who had hired his father-in-law to coach the team. The Warriors retaliated by obtaining a court order that prevented Barry for playing in the ABA for one year, so he spent the 1967–68 campaign as the team's broadcaster. The ABA did manage to sign New Mexico State center Mel Daniels and Clemson forward Randy Mahaffey—both of whom had been selected in the first round of the NBA draft—and All-American guards Louie Dampier, Bob Verga, and Bobby Lloyd. The ABA also accepted four players who had been banned by the NBA for their alleged involvement in the 1961 college betting scandals: Roger Brown, Doug Moe, Tony Jackson, and Connie Hawkins.

The league's first season was notable for small crowds and big performances. Among the best players were Moe and his New Orleans teammate Larry Brown; Daniels, who led the ABA in rebounding; and Hawkins, who led the league in scoring, won the MVP award, and led his Pittsburgh Pipers to a spectacular seven-game victory over New Orleans in the ABA championship series.

Two More for Old Time's Sake

In the NBA, the 1967–68 regular season went more or less as expected. Chamberlain continued to collect around 24 points and

THE HAWK

Given all of the strides made by the NBA during the 1960s, it is worth noting that the player considered by many to be the game's most exciting was actually blackballed until he was well past his prime. Connie Hawkins, perhaps the finest athlete ever to come out of the Brooklyn playgrounds, had it all. He stood 6'8", had great ballhandling and leaping ability, and could shoot from 25 feet. A monster rebounder and shot-blocker, he liked to leave his special mark—both offensively and defensively—on every game he played. While still in high school he played Wilt Chamberlain in a one-on-one and nearly beat him.

Given a scholarship to the University of Iowa in 1960, the naive and inexperienced Hawkins found himself an unfortunate pawn in a betting scandal. Led to believe that he was cooperating with investigators, he actually incriminated himself and was kicked out of college and subsequently banned from the NBA. Over the next seven years he survived on basketball's fringes, playing for the Pittsburgh Rens of the short-lived American Basketball League (he won the MVP award) and performing with the Harlem Globetrotters for a time. In 1967, he signed with the Pittsburgh Pipers of the American Basketball Association and had a spectacular season. The Pipers won the ABA title and Hawkins was the league's MVP, but "Hawk" still yearned to play in the NBA.

He finally got his chance after suing the NBA. The league settled out of court and permitted Hawkins to join the Phoenix Suns. He responded with a 24.6 scoring average and made first-team All-NBA. Despite his remarkable numbers, Hawkins was by this time a mere shadow of his former self. Chronic knee problems had robbed him of his jumping and cutting ability, stealing from Hawkins the most vital part of his game. Even so, he appeared in four All-Star games and finished his NBA career with an average of 18.9 points per game.

Connie Hawkins, whose one-on-one artistry and heart-stopping aerial maneuvers made him a Brooklyn playground legend. A college betting scandal kept him out of the pro-basketball limelight for years, but he had several good years after joining the NBA's Phoenix Suns in 1969.

24 rebounds a game, and actually improved his passing to the point where he topped the league with 702 assists. Of all the records Chamberlain set during his career, this might be the one with the best chance of lasting forever—the chances of someone averaging 50 points a game again seem a lot better than the prospect of another center leading the NBA in assists. The 76ers eclipsed the 60-win mark for the second straight season, finishing eight games ahead of the aging Celtics. As the season wore on and the injuries mounted, Bill Russell had to go deep into his bench. But the grade-A subs of past years were nowhere to be found. Still, Russell was able to will 54 victories out of this group—a feat of which few took notice as the postseason began.

The Celtics breezed through the first round against the improved Detroit Pistons, who boasted a trio of good young players in forwards Dave DeBusschere and Happy Hairston, and high-scoring guard Dave Bing. The 76ers played another good young team, the New York Knicks, whose season had been transformed when Red Holzman took over the coaching role 38 games into the season. What had formerly been an ineffective hodgepodge of promising players—including big men Walt Bellamy and Willis Reed, forwards Cazzie Russell and Bill Bradley, and guards Walt Frazier and Dick Barnett—turned into a tight, smart unit that moved the ball quickly on offense and played tough defense. The Knicks nearly stole the series from Philadelphia, and in the process knocked Billy Cunningham out of the 76er lineup for the remainder of the postseason. When the Celtics and 76ers met in the semifinals, it was all Philadelphia at first, as the Sixers took a 3–1 lead. The Celtics staved off elimination in Philly, then knotted the series at 3–3 in their own building. The seventh game, played in Philadelphia, saw the 76ers suffer through an uncharacteristic shooting slump. Without Cunningham's instant offense off the bench, they found themselves down a basket with less than a minute to play. Russell took over, batting away Chet Walker's shot and snaring the rebound off a Hal Greer miss and gunning it to Sam Jones, who put the game

The unstoppable Wilt Chamberlain meets the indomitable Bill Russell in a game in Boston Garden. The legendary battles between the two centers were the NBA's prime attraction during the 1960s.

THE THREE-POINT BOMB

When the American Basketball Association was being formed, the league needed something more than a red-white-and-blue basketball to distinguish itself from the NBA. From the very start, everyone involved agreed that the three-point play, an idea first employed in Abe Saperstein's short-lived American Basketball League, would do the trick. The idea was to stretch the defenses out so that the ABA's more athletic players could shine. The three-pointer would also give an advantage to the smaller guards who tended to sign with the ABA.

While coaches took a while to get used to the three-pointer, the players had no problem at all. The Kentucky Colonels had a pair of bombers in guards Louie Dampier and Darel Carrier, and they quickly became the league's long-distance "specialists." One player, Les Selvage, liked the three-point shot so much that he was known to pull up on fast breaks so he could fire away from 25 feet. In his first season with the Anaheim Amigos he attempted 461 three-pointers, and in a game against Denver he attempted 26 of them. Selvage did not last long in the pros—he was cut the following year and played a week for the Los Angeles Stars two seasons later—but he is fondly remembered by ABA old-timers.

Eventually, ABA coaches, players, and fans came to understand how best to use the three-pointer, and it became an important part of the league's playing style. When the leagues merged in 1976, NBA executives lobbied against the three-point shot, with Boston's Red Auerbach among its most vocal opponents. After the Celtics drafted Larry Bird, however, Auerbach suddenly reversed his stand and was a major reason the rule was pushed through. Since then, the three-pointer has had a profound impact on how NBA basketball is both coached and played.

away. In the finals, the Los Angeles Lakers went down to their sixth straight defeat against the Celtics, 4 games to 2. Against all odds, Boston had won yet another championship. And the Lakers had blown it again.

A few weeks later, Los Angeles got what everyone assumed was the puzzle piece it had always been missing. Alex Hannum resigned his post in Philadelphia to coach Rick Barry in the ABA, and his replacement, Jack Ramsay, announced that the 76ers would become strictly a running team. This meant Chamberlain (history's all-time best half-court player) would be available. Ramsay wanted a good young guard and a serviceable center, which the Lakers had. So L.A. got Chamberlain for Archie Clark, an excellent playmaker, and Darrall Imhoff, who had earned NBA All-Star honors in 1967. With Chamberlain, Jerry West, and Elgin Baylor, the Lakers had three of the best players on the planet. If by some miracle the Celtics managed to sneak into the finals again, Los Angeles would surely kill them.

Boston had an uphill climb to return to the finals, even with Chamberlain in the Western Conference. The 76ers were flourishing under Ramsay, while the Knicks had become even better after Dave DeBusschere was obtained in a December trade for Bellamy and Reed was shifted into the center position. The big surprise in the East, however, was Baltimore. The Bullets improved by 21 wins over the year before and went from worst to first thanks to the arrival of a 6'7" rookie center named Wes Unseld. One of basketball's original "widebodies," Unseld planted himself in the lane like an oak tree and punished opposing centers. His ability to clear the boards and fire long passes downcourt turned a team of good shooters (including Earl Monroe, Jack Marin, and Kevin Loughery) into an unstoppable fast-break machine.

Trailing these three dynamic young teams were the Celtics, whose eight-man rotation averaged 32 years old. Putting even more strain on player-coach Russell was that his longtime backup, Wayne Embry, quit basketball to become Recreation Commissioner for the City of Boston. Embry's replacement, Jim ("Bad News") Barnes, was so bad that Russell kept himself in games for an average of 43 minutes—far longer than anyone else on the team. Not surprisingly, over the last half of the season, Boston failed to win even half its games. The Celtic dynasty seemed to be done.

The playoffs began in startling fashion, as the Knicks wiped out the Bullets in four straight games, and the Celtics got past the 76ers with relative ease. In the division final, the veteran Celtics tricked the inexperienced Knicks into throwing away the first two games and then held on to split the next four. In the West, the Lakers breezed to the finals with wins over the San Francisco Warriors and newly relocated Atlanta Hawks. Thus the 1969 NBA Finals found the creaky Celtics going up against Chamberlain, West, and Baylor.

Facing almost certain defeat, Russell knew he needed an imaginative plan of attack. He benched starting guard Larry Siegfried in favor of Emmett Bryant, who was much quicker defensively. He encouraged Sam Jones and John Havlicek to pick up the scoring slack, and implored Bailey Howell to make the 34-year-old Baylor work hard for every bucket. Russell would do his best to control Chamberlain, and they would pray that West had a couple of off nights. In the opener, Russell's plan worked well except for one crucial detail: West lit up the Celtics for 53 points and dealt out 10 assists. In Game 2, West hit for 41, and the Lakers won again.

Los Angeles nearly took a 3–0 lead back at the Boston Garden, when Keith Erickson poked John Havlicek in the eye. "Hondo" played with one eye shut and scored 34, including the deciding free throws, and Boston was back in it. In the fourth game, the Celtics finally neutralized West, but still trailed 88-87 with 15 seconds left. The Lakers had the ball and could have easily run out the clock, but Bryant came through with a steal and the Celtics were able to set up a final shot. An intricate triple-screen gave Jones shooting room from 18 feet with three seconds remaining; he slipped as he shot and fell backwards, and then the Lakers could only watch as the improbable shot hit the front rim, popped up, hit the back rim, and then settled into the basket as the buzzer sounded. The Lakers regained some momentum with a Game 5 win, as Chamberlain limited Russell to just two points and

West scored 39, but Russell returned the favor in Game 6, holding Wilt to a single basket in a nine-point Boston win.

When Jerry West, nursing a hamstring pull that had occurred earlier in the series, walked out onto the L.A. Forum floor to play Game 7, he immediately saw that Lakers owner Jack Kent Cooke had made a terrible mistake. With Cooke's assent, thousands of balloons had been strung up in nets among the buildings rafters, in anticipation of a Laker victory and championship celebration. Everyone knew the Celtics were running on empty, but West immediately knew that Russell would use those balloons to incite and inspire his players. The Celtics opened up a big lead in the third quarter, but Russell and Jones had five fouls. Chamberlain also had been whistled for five, and he was in no mood to foul out. As these three stars played tentatively, West exploded to make the game close again.

As the fourth quarter passed its midway point, Jones had fouled out and Havlicek picked up his fifth foul. The Celtics had nothing left and were holding on for dear life. They got a break when, with 5:45 left, Chamberlain left the game after wrenching his knee. West continued to dominate, bringing the Lakers within a single point at 103-102 with three minutes to play. Chamberlain asked to go back in, but coach Butch Van Breda Kolff (in a move that infuriates Wilt to this day) told him to sit down—the Lakers were doing fine without him. With a minute left and Chamberlain watching from the bench, Don Nelson hit a prayer from the foul line that put the Celtics ahead by three, and the game went to Boston 108-106. It was the most controversial, touching, and spectacular final ever played, and a fitting tribute to Russell, who announced his retirement that summer. The Celtic dynasty had ended as it begun: with a hair-raising, two-point, Game 7 victory.

The Wooden Years

The 1966 NCAA Tournament, distinguished by the landmark victory of an all-black Texas Western squad over an all-white Kentucky team, also marked the one and only time between 1964 and 1975 that the University of California at Los Angeles did not make the "Final Four." UCLA, coached by John Wooden, dominated this era as no college team has before or since. The "Wizard of Westwood" led the Bruins to a 335–21 record over those 12 seasons, including a record 88 wins in a row. Ten times UCLA advanced to the NCAA final, and each time the Bruins won. In four of those years, the team completed the season with a 30–0 record.

Wooden was a master at bringing the right kind of players into his system and in-

John Wooden at work during a time-out huddle. The "Wizard of Westwood" coached his UCLA Bruins to an incredible 10 NCAA championships in a span of 12 years.

stilling in them the belief that they could not be beaten if they followed his instructions. What is interesting is that the instructions Wooden gave varied from team to team depending on the personnel, and from game to game depending on the opponent. It was an interesting approach for a coach in any sport. Instead of concentrating on one style, he drilled his players in a number of different styles. Then he asked them to trust him as he switched strategies, often from one possession to the next. A coach playing UCLA during the Wooden years knew exactly what to expect: an offense and defense designed specifically to beat him. How could anyone win against that kind of team?

Wooden's players had to play smart, aggressive defense and look to break the other way once they gained possession of the ball. Like any coach, Wooden preferred to build his team around one or two superstars, but what separated him from his peers is that he could produce a dominant team without a marquee player. In the 1964 final against Duke, for instance, it was swingman Kenny Washington who quadrupled his season average and scored 26 points to sink the bewildered Blue Devils.

The first two Wooden champions were guard-oriented teams. Sharp-shooting Gail Goodrich and Walt Hazzard led the way in 1964; Goodrich flew solo in 1965 after Hazzard graduated. The 1965 final saw Goodrich take command of a slightly weaker Bruin squad and shred the vaunted University of Michigan defense for 42 points. In what Wooden called the greatest clutch performance he ever saw, the 6'1" guard fouled out three of the top defenders in the country in a stunning 91-80 win.

Wooden's 1965–66 team went 18–8 but failed to make the NCAA draw because they were not the best team in their conference. It may sound crazy, but the 1966 Bruins were not even the best team on their own campus that year. The UCLA freshman team featured guards Lucius Allen and Ken Heitz and forward Lynn Shackelford—each among the most heavily recruited high-schoolers in the country the year before. In the middle was 7'1" Lew Alcindor, who averaged 31 points and 21 rebounds to lead the UCLA frosh to a perfect 21–0 record. That mark would have been 22–0 had the game against the UCLA varsity counted. In that contest Alcindor and company whipped the upperclassmen 75-60!

The 1966–67 season started off with Alcindor scoring 56 points in his varsity debut, and later that year he hit for 61 in a game against Washington State. Basketball had come a long way in the decade since Wilt Chamberlain wreaked havoc in college—there were more and better big men, and coaches had devised special defenses to deal with seven-footers. But Alcindor was every bit as dominant as Wilt had been. His "sky hook" was the most indefensible move in the history of the game, a hook shot he released—accurately with either hand—at the apex of his considerable leap, from somewhere well above the rim. Behind their sophomore sensation, the Bruins rolled to a perfect season and whipped the University of Dayton in the NCAA final to begin a seven-year string of national titles.

Wooden's greatest challenge came in the years after Alcindor graduated. Without a dominant man in the middle, some believed the "Wizard of Westwood" would be unable to keep the UCLA streak alive. But they had forgotten the great pre-Alcindor teams, which relied on intelligence and conditioning to pull out games when no superstar stepped up to lead the charge. In Alcindor's last year, the team had a pair of first-year forwards named Curtis Rowe and Sidney Wicks. Both could shoot, rebound, and play defense—all that Wooden ever required of his players. Guard John Valley and center Steve Patterson came through after spending a couple of seasons on the bench, and sophomore Henry Bibby provided clutch outside shooting.

The Bruins came into the 1970 NCAA Tournament ranked behind Adolph Rupp's Kentucky squad, but never faced the Wildcats—Kentucky lost to Artis Gilmore and the University of Jacksonville. The 7'2" center made the Dolphins hard to beat; that season Jacksonville led the nation in points per game, shooting percentage, and average margin of victory. In the final, Wooden put Wicks on Gilmore despite a six-inch height differential. The junior responded by swatting five Gilmore shots and totally demoralizing Jacksonville to take a fourth straight national title. The Bruins won it all again in 1970–71, with benchwarmers Terry Schofield and Kenny Booker filling in for the departed Valley.

The wins kept coming in 1971–72, as center Bill Walton joined the team. Walton was the best-passing big man the college game had ever seen and Wooden made excellent use of this added dimension, surrounding his center with quick cutters and accurate shooters. Bibby was joined by sophomore Keith Wilkes, giving Walton a couple of scorers to whom he could dish off when double-teamed. The Bruins went 30–0, and never trailed in a game by more than seven points all season long. For his part, Walton became the first player since Oscar Robertson to be named NCAA Player of the Year in his first varsity season.

The "Walton Gang" turned in another perfect season in 1972–73, marking the first time a major college had ever had gone unbeaten two years in a row. This squad featured the best front court in college history. Walton improved his play in every area, while Wilkes and senior forward Larry Farmer hit more than half their shots from the floor. Coming off the bench were center Swen Nater and forward Dave Meyers, each of whom would go on to star in the pros. In the NCAA final against Memphis State University, Walton played the game of his life, canning 21 of 22 shots to finish with 44 points.

UCLA's winning streak ended at 88 games the next season, and the Bruins got bumped out of the NCAA Tournament by David Thompson and North Carolina State University. It was the first time in 39 NCAA contests that UCLA had lost, and it took two overtimes to do it. The following season, Wooden called it quits, but he went out in typical style. Coaching a team that lacked a big man and a shooting guard, he nevertheless managed to guide the Bruins into the NCAA Tournament with a sparkling 23–3 record. Whether by coincidence or design, almost every game the Bruins played featured a poor performance by the opposition's star player. When it was all said and done, though, UCLA stood atop the college basketball world once again. If ever there was a time when the UCLA "mystique" contributed to a Bruin championship this was clearly it.

From 1967 to 1975, there was little suspense to the college basketball season, except to see which school would earn the privilege of being clobbered by UCLA. This situation did not dampen enthusiasm for college basketball—if anything, it drew more attention to it. Sports fans flocked to their television sets for college games, not just to see Alcindor, Walton, and their cohorts, but to check on the new generation of stars. In 1972, the

NCAA reversed its policy banning freshman from varsity play, and this greatly strengthened the depth and quality of college ball. Hot-shot high-school players started signing with schools that would give them a chance start right away, and this had an interesting effect on the balance of power. Schools such as UCLA and Kentucky—where it had long been considered an honor to sit on the bench for a couple of years—had trouble talking the top recruits into starting their college careers as backups. Conversely, schools that had never been in the running for these players could now promise an opportunity to start for four years, with a chance to develop and showcase their skills for the pros. With the talent spread so evenly throughout the country, it became impossible for a team to build a dynasty like UCLA's. And with so many players getting a chance to shine, the college

THE BIG E

The only player who put a scare into John Wooden's Bruins was Elvin Hayes of the University of Houston. Though shorter than Lew Alcindor at 6'9", the "Big E" was a strong rebounder and defender, and had an array of offensive moves—including a deadly baseline fadeaway—that in many ways surpassed Alcindor's. A consistent 25-point scorer, Hayes led a loose and creative Cougar team that coach Guy Lewis allowed to freelance on offense. Defensively, Houston was excellent, with Don Chaney, a big aggressive guard, keeping opponents from operating freely on the outside and Hayes stuffing anything that came near the basket. In the 1967 NCAA Tournament, Hayes and Alcindor played to a standoff during their first meeting, although UCLA won by 15. The rematch occurred the following season at the Houston Astrodome, in front of 55,000 fans and millions of TV viewers. The Bruins were riding a 47-game winning streak, but Alcindor had gotten scratched in the eye two games earlier and was not really 100 percent. That small difference was all Hayes needed, as he burned the Bruin front line for 39 points in a wild 71-69 win. When the teams met again—in the NCAA semifinals—Wooden devised a special anti-Hayes "diamond-and-one" defense that put forward Lynn Shackelford on Houston's star all game long. The Bruins won by 32 points, and rubbed it in by playing their subs for a significant portion of the second half.

Elvin Hayes elevates over Lew Alcindor for a bucket during Houston's stunning 71-69 upset of UCLA in January 1968.

game had more young stars and "Cinderella" teams than ever before.

Among the great college stars who shared the spotlight with John Wooden's UCLA Bruins was a quintet of big guards and small forwards: Bill Bradley, Cazzie Russell, Rick Mount, Pete Maravich, Austin Carr, and David Thompson. Bradley brought respect back to Ivy League basketball when he led Princeton University to the Final Four in 1965, scored a record 58 points in a NCAA Tournament game, and was named national Player of the Year. A tireless worker both on and off the court, he was a good player who made himself great. Bradley's offensive skills were enough to earn a scholarship from any school in the country, but his grades were good enough to get into Princeton, one of the top universities in the world. Once there he became the consummate team player, making his teammates better and then picking up the slack when they got in over their heads. Bradley averaged 30 points and 12 rebounds a game in college, and led the Tigers to three Ivy League titles.

Princeton's Bill Bradley goes to the hole against Michigan's Cazzie Russell during their famous 1964 Holiday Tournament battle. Both men went on to play important roles on the New York Knicks' 1970 championship team, and Bradley later became a U.S. Senator.

Bradley's arch rival, Russell, supplied the points for the University of Michigan and was Player of the Year in 1966. A three-time All-American, Russell was a big guard who could score points in bunches, either from the outside or down the middle, where he regularly challenged forwards and centers. He patterned his game after Oscar Robertson's, although he never acquired the Big O's liking for defense. His most famous game came against Bradley at the 1964 Holiday Tournament. "Dollar Bill" hit for 41 and gave Princeton a 13-point lead before fouling out, but then Russell brought the Wolverines charging back for a thrilling 80-78 win. Ironically, both men were drafted by the New York Knicks and were key contributors to New York's 1970 NBA championship.

Mount, the first high-school player ever to make the cover of *Sports Illustrated,* was a national celebrity before he even took a shot for the Purdue Boilermakers. A pure shooter, he poured in points from the guard position, almost always topping 30 a game. In his varsity debut, he nearly beat Lew Alcindor and the UCLA Bruins, and in his junior year he carried an otherwise unremarkable Boilermaker squad to the NCAA final.

Every bit Mount's equal as a scorer—and then some—was Pete Maravich of Louisiana State University. Playing guard for his father, Press, "Pistol Pete" was instructed to put the ball up whenever he got a good look at the basket. The result was an average of 44.2 points per game over 83 career contests, including 60 or more against Tulane University, the University of Alabama, Vanderbilt University, and Kentucky. A unanimous first-team All-American in each of his three varsity seasons, Maravich was more than just a great shooter. He was the game's most accomplished ball handler and, on those rare occasions when he passed the ball, he was an excellent assist man. He was named College Player of the Year in 1970, and left LSU with 11 NCAA records and 26 Southeast Conference marks. Following Maravich as the nation's top player in 1971 was Notre Dame's Austin Carr. He scored 38 points a game in his junior and senior seasons, hitting from the outside and driving to the basket. An excellent player off the ball, the 6'4" Carr often snagged 10 rebounds a game. On defense, he usually drew the other team's toughest guard.

"Pistol Pete" Maravich flips in a reverse layup during the game that saw him break the record for most career points scored by a college player. He averaged a whopping 44.2 points per game over his career at LSU.

Thompson, who also stood 6'4", joined the North Carolina State University varsity in 1972–73 and quite literally took the "big guard" position to new heights. Using an explosive first step and eye-popping jumping ability, Thompson made the dunk shot a lethal weapon—something it had never been for a backcourt player. When double-teamed, he would simply rise gracefully into the air and fire a jumper high over the outstretched arms of his defenders. Thompson was virtually automatic for 30 points a game from the day he walked on a college basketball court, and he earned All-America honors in each of his three varsity seasons. As a sophomore he led N.C. State to a perfect 27–0 record, and in 1973–74 he went right at UCLA's Bill Walton and beat the Bruins in the NCAA semifinals. Two days later he led the Wolfpack to the national title with an easy win over Marquette. Considered the nation's finest player in 1974 and 1975, Thompson made a lot of people appreciate just how far college basketball had come in 30 years since Kenny Sailors unveiled his radical new jumper in Madison Square Garden.

The Playground Game Goes Big-Time

A snapshot of professional basketball in the spring of 1970 shows just how much the game had changed in only 10 years. The NBA had gone from 8 teams to 14, with plans to add 3 more the following fall. The ABA had completed its second season with 11 franchises, bringing to 28 the total number of pro teams at the beginning of the decade. The starting five for each of the NBA's six best teams included either three or four black players. The $100,000 salary—considered a dream in 1960—was not only a reality, but soon would be considered "chump change" as competition between the two leagues heated up.

The game was also being played more and more above the rim. An influx of shifty ball handlers during the 1960s had been countered by an overall improvement in defense, but a player with a three-foot vertical leap could simply rise above the average defender—a fact that more and more coaches were beginning to realize. Another interesting shift spurred by the heightened quality of players coming into the pros was that the role for each position was beginning to change. Point guards were shooting more, while shooting guards were slicing inside and dunking the ball; shooting forwards were handling the ball out on the perimeter, while power forwards were backing out of the paint and letting the ball go from 12 to 15 feet. The center position, however, remained more or less the same. If a team had a great center, it built its game plan around him—if not, it tried to maximize his strengths and mask his weaknesses.

The NBA continued to prize well-rounded ballplayers—team players, who could score within the flow of a patterned offense, and who worked just as hard at defending and rebounding as they did at getting their own shots. The ABA owners, on the other hand, thought of their league as show business, and they wanted players who could draw fans into their arenas, and then make them leap out of their seats. What the ABA did was give a national stage to the free-flowing basketball genius of the inner-city playground game.

The playground game had a different set of values than the basketball on display at major colleges and in the NBA. Style and creativity—one-handed rebounds, flashy ball-handling, unique and high-flying dunks—were the qualities that cemented a playground player's reputation. While these kinds of moves made old-guard NBA coaches cringe, many fans loved these new one-on-one artists—they dribbled, spun, slashed, jumped, and double-clutched their way to the hoop, regardless of how many defenders they had to go through to get there.

Although few basketball fans realized it at the time, the wide-open style of the ABA would prove very important to the evolution of basketball. The game was getting very sophisticated, and coaches were finding it easier to neutralize the kind of players who had been successful during the 1960s. Without the experimentation that was possible in the new league, pro ball would have stagnated. And do-it-all players like Michael Jordan, who have the ability to single-handedly break down almost any defense, owe a lot of their moves to the pioneering stars of the ABA.

The ABA owners bargained hard for the services of UCLA superstar Lew Alcindor and LSU's Pete Maravich, but lost both to the NBA. The ABA snared teen star Spencer Haywood by drafting him after his sophomore year—claiming that his family was experiencing financial hardship—and set a precedent that enabled the league to sign Julius Erving, Ralph Simpson, Jim Chones, Brian Taylor, and Johnny Neumann before they were eligible to play in the NBA. The ABA also continued to raid the NBA for established players. The Oakland Oaks moved to Washington and signed Dave Bing to a future deal, and the Carolina Cougars did the same with Billy Cunningham. Cunningham would join the team after he played out his option with the 76ers and go on to win the ABA MVP, but the Bing deal fell through. Several NBA first-rounders went with ABA clubs, including Artis Gilmore, Jim McDaniels, Larry Cannon, Dan Issel, Charlie Scott, and Rick Mount. Among the less-publicized but highly talented players who signed with ABA teams during the league's first few seasons were Ron Boone, George McGinnis, Mack Calvin, Rich Jones, George Carter, John Brisker, and Willie Wise—any one of whom could have started in the NBA.

Julius Erving turned out to be the prize catch. A one-man team at the University of Massachusetts, he was not well known among hoops fans but the pro scouts were well aware of his abilities. He reminded many of Elgin Baylor, but he was even smoother and could hang in the air even longer. He had the fluid moves and ballhandling skills of a smaller man, much as Connie Hawkins had displayed during his years on basketball's fringes during the 1960s. And "Dr. J," as he liked to be called, could also pass, defend, and rebound. The NBA did not have a forward who could take a game by the throat and make it his own, which was why the ABA was willing to pay Erving well for his services. He declared

The true standard-bearer for the flamboyant ABA game turned out to be Julius Erving. "Dr. J" dominated the league and electrified fans with his high-flying creativity—by all accounts, no one has ever played the game with as much style.

himself eligible after his junior year and signed a four-year pact with the Virginia Squires for $500,000.

After one season with the Squires, Erving was the ABA's top player and number-one gate attraction. He realized that he had sold himself short, and approached the Atlanta Hawks, who had acquired his rights in the 1972 NBA draft. Erving signed with Atlanta and actually suited up for an exhibition game, but the courts upheld Virginia's insistence that he honor his original contract. Irritated with their superstar, the Squires dealt him to the New York Nets, who had just lost Rick Barry. Barry had similar misgivings about the ABA and decided to return to the NBA Warriors.

The Indiana Pacers were usually the class of the ABA, winning three championships in the league's first six years.

Over the next three seasons Erving fulfilled his commitment and stuck with the ABA, establishing himself as the most breathtaking basketball player anyone had ever seen. He led the league in scoring in 1973–74 and 1975–76, won the MVP in each season, and led the Nets to a pair of ABA championships. Erving also made the fans jump out of their seats—something that was happening less and less at NBA games.

For all of its undisciplined play, the ABA did have one highly disciplined team. The Indiana Pacers, under coach Slick Leonard, were a balanced, intelligent squad with a mix of stars and role players that rivaled any group the NBA could offer. Mel Daniels, an ABA original, played center and dominated opponents under the boards. He was the main reason the Pacers won three league titles, and he was twice named ABA MVP. The Pacer scoring punch was supplied by George McGinnis and Roger Brown. McGinnis was a burly, chain-smoking forward with a quirky one-handed jumper. He was already an Indiana hero by the time he came to the Pacers, having eclipsed Oscar Robertson's schoolboy scoring record. He played one season for Indiana University and then signed with the Pacers in 1971, and led the team to two ABA titles. Brown, who moved easily from guard to forward, was the first player signed by Indiana. Banned from the NBA, he played for industrial league teams for several years before getting his chance in the ABA. A remarkable long-distance shooter, Brown was the league's premier pressure player. In the 1970 ABA finals, he burned the Los Angeles Stars for 53 and 45 points in the clinching games. Meanwhile, Brown's buzzer-beaters became an ABA staple. As a clutch shooter he rivaled Jerry West, and in the final minute of close games, Indiana fans would start chanting *Roger! Roger! Roger!* The Pacers were, by every conceivable measure, the class of the ABA. They amassed more victories, won more titles, and drew more fans than any other franchise.

Escalating salaries, the exploding popularity of college basketball, and the lack of a national television contract ultimately doomed the ABA. By the end of the 1975–76 season, the league was in a shambles. Still, the ABA had some of the game's most exciting players. In its final season, the league boasted guards David Thompson, George Gervin, John Williamson, and Don Buse, forwards Julius Erving, Dan Issel, Bobby Jones, Billy Knight, Larry Kenon, Maurice Lucas, Caldwell Jones, Dan Roundfield, and M. L. Carr, and centers Swen Nater, Marvin Webster, Artis Gilmore, and Moses Malone.

Obviously, this was worth something to the NBA. The league agreed to expand, absorbing the Nets, Nuggets, Pacers, and Spurs. The remaining players were distributed among the other league franchises. The merger not only consolidated pro basketball's talent pool, but reinvigorated the NBA, which was starting to play a sluggish, defense-oriented style of ball. The impact of this new talent was profound: The following season, two of the top five NBA scorers, shooters, and rebounders were former ABAers, and Buse led the league in assists. Four of the top five offensive rebounders were also former ABA stars.

In the seven seasons following the merger, the NBA MVP award was won by a former ABA player four times, and 15 of the 35 spots on the All-NBA first team went to ex-ABA stars. As for the notion that no one in the ABA played defense, during the same seven-year span no fewer than 18 spots on the NBA's All-Defensive first team went to ABA alumni. Looking beyond the years following the merger, the ABA's impact might have been even more profound. Between the defunct league's playing style and three-point rule (which was adopted by the NBA a couple of years later), today's professional game looks a lot more like a 1975 ABA game than a 1975 NBA contest!

Stars of the 1970s

The NBA during the 1970s was a far better league, of course. And given how tough it

Despite his tremendous all-around skills, Oscar Robertson could never get his Cincinnati Royals teams of the 1960s past Bill Russell and Wilt Chamberlain in the playoffs. The "Big O" finally got over the hump in 1971 with the Milwaukee Bucks as he and Lew Alcindor led the team to a 66–16 record and a championship.

had become just to stay in the lineup, the stars that emerged during this period deserve a lot more respect than they are sometimes given. Because of the rising quality of play, someone with a glaring deficiency could be exploited quite effectively. There were, for instance, several great shooters in the league who probably would have flourished in the ABA, but they remained on NBA benches for the balance of games because they happened to be below-average defenders. In the old days, these individuals could have been matched up against a second-rate offensive player on the other team, but not anymore. As the 20-point scorers on NBA expansion teams proved, there were plenty of guys who could put the ball in the hole, but if they allowed their man to come back with 25 or 30, they were not much use to a contending team. It is highly probable that many of the top scorers of the 1960s would not have started in the NBA of the 1970s for precisely this reason. Indeed, most of the 1960s stars who played on into the 1970s found themselves demoted to utility roles.

The top players in the NBA before the league merged and expanded were distributed fairly evenly across all the positions. The best young centers were Dave Cowens, Bob Lanier, and Lew Alcindor, who changed his name to Kareem Abdul-Jabbar after converting to Islam. Cowens reminded many of Bill Russell, the man he succeeded in the Boston pivot. He stood 6'9", was a tenacious rebounder, and he never gave up on defense. Cowens could also do something Russell could not: shoot from the outside. This skill opened up defenses for Celtic drivers like John Havlicek, Don Nelson, and Jo Jo White, and enabled the team's best rebounder, Paul Silas, to work the boards with great effectiveness. With Cowens as its centerpiece, Boston returned to glory and won NBA titles in 1974 and 1976. Lanier, though more of a classic center in terms of size and skills, was also an excellent outside shooter. He did his best work for the lackluster Detroit Pistons, then moved on to Milwaukee in 1980, where he led the Bucks to five straight division titles

Dave Cowens rips a rebound away from Julius Erving. A bulldog on the boards and on defense, Cowens also had an improbably soft shooting touch, and he led the Celtics back to glory in 1974 and 1976.

before a seventh knee operation cut him down in 1984.

Abdul-Jabbar, meanwhile, went from being the game's top college player to establishing himself as the best in the pros. Although he faced better defenders than he had in college, Abdul-Jabbar continued to score and rebound at an astounding clip. And the lessons he took from UCLA helped him become an excellent team player. In his second NBA season, he teamed with veteran Oscar Robertson and young forwards Bob Dandridge and Greg Smith to lead the Milwaukee Bucks to 66 regular-season victories; the Bucks then roared past the Warriors, Lakers, and Bullets to win the NBA championship. The Bucks went 12–2 in the playoffs, as Abdul-Jabbar outdueled Nate Thurmond, Wilt Chamberlain, and Wes Unseld—the three top veteran centers in basketball. An ill-advised trade in 1975 sent him to the Los Angeles Lakers, who were rebuilding after the departures of Chamberlain, West, and Hairston. Kareem played out his career in L.A., becoming the centerpiece of one of history's most colorful and dynamic teams during the 1980s.

Kareem Abdul-Jabbar shoots the skyhook—perhaps the most lethal move basketball has ever seen—over Boston's Don Nelson.

Among the NBA's top forwards were Elvin Hayes, Bob Love, Rick Barry, Dave DeBusschere, and Havlicek. Hayes went to the San Diego Rockets in the 1968 expansion draft, and he led the league in scoring as a rookie. The Big E was the NBA's top rebounder in his second season, but the team failed to win and he was traded to the Bullets after the 1971–72 campaign. In Baltimore (and later, when the team moved to Washington), Hayes was surrounded by a number of excellent all-around players, such as Phil Chenier, Dave Bing, Archie Clark, Wes Unseld, and Truck Robinson. This freed him to crash the boards and take the big shots, without the burden of having to score 30 points a game. Hayes and the Bullets flourished after the trade, and they went to the NBA finals two years in a row at the end of the 1970s. Love provided the scoring for a Chicago Bulls team which specialized in rugged defense. A silky-smooth shooter, he averaged between 21 and 25 points a game for six years in a row, and led the Bulls to 50-win seasons from 1970–71 to 1973–74.

Barry, DeBusschere, and Havlicek, of course, were All-Stars during the 1960s, but their stars shone all the more brightly during the 1970s. Barry returned from the ABA in 1972–73 and made first-team All-NBA three years in a row. His outside shooting and passing were even better than when he had left, and although he was reviled by the

Lightning-quick point guard Nate ("Tiny") Archibald—pictured here on a Topps trading card—had a season for the ages in 1972–73, averaging 11.4 assists and a cool 34 points per game—both league-leading figures.

NBA establishment for jumping to the ABA, he remained a fan favorite with his long-range bombing, fancy playmaking, and underhand free throws. Barry was the centerpiece of the 1974–75 Golden State Warriors, who surprised everybody by winning the Pacific Division in what was supposed to have been a rebuilding year, then working their way through the playoffs and eventually sweeping the heavily favored Baltimore Bullets in the Finals.

DeBusschere was the prototype of the modern power forward. He played great position defense, went to the boards hard, and could score from the perimeter. A brief stint as a player-coach with the Pistons in the 1960s prepared him for life as a New York Knick under coach Red Holzman, who preached ball movement on offense and teamwork on defense. DeBusschere was a key figure in the two championships won by the Knicks during the 1970s, and made the NBA's All-Defensive first team every year from 1969 until he retired in 1974. Havlicek, meanwhile, found life with the "new" Celtics very much to his liking. In the five seasons following the retirement of Bill Russell and Sam Jones, "Hondo" was the Celts' go-to guy and boosted his assist and rebounding numbers, consistently scored in the mid-20s, and made the league's All-Defensive first team every year from 1972 to 1976.

The 1970s saw several great guards come to prominence. Chief among them were Walt Frazier, Nate Archibald, Calvin Murphy, and Jo Jo White. Frazier was basketball's coolest player, both on and off the court. He ran the Knick offense and took the team's clutch shots, while playing outstanding defense. A big man with flashy ballhandling skills and a ball fake that got even the best defenders flying in the air, Frazier surpassed Jerry West in the early 1970s as the supreme all-around guard in the league. Nicknamed Clyde because his style of dress reminded some of an old-time gangster, he was as fearless a player in big games as has ever set foot on the hardwood.

Archibald did not have the good fortune to play on a top team until the downside of his career, when he joined the Celtics in the late 1970s. As the point guard for the lowly Kings, he was expected to pass the ball to his teammates or shoot it himself virtually every time down the court. He did both with great effectiveness and enthusiasm, becoming the only player ever to lead the league in scoring and assists in the same season. A typical performance for Tiny was 30 points and 10 as-

TITLE TIME FOR NEW YORK AND L.A.

With the Celtic stranglehold on the NBA finals broken, the way was clear for some interesting new teams to compete for the championship. The New York Knicks brought together an intriguing mix of players and won championships in 1970 and 1973. They did so by playing unselfish basketball and maximizing the talents of their roster, which included (at various times) Willis Reed, Dave DeBusschere, Bill Bradley, Jerry Lucas, Cazzie Russell, Dave Stallworth, Walt Frazier, Dick Barnett, Mike Riordan, and Earl Monroe. Any one of these players could have averaged 20 to 25 points a game for another team, but each chose to work within coach Holzman's system. The 1970 championship, won in seven games against the Lakers, was particularly sweet for veterans Reed and Barnett, who had toiled unappreciated for most of the 1960s. The 1973 title was the high point for Lucas, who had failed to win with Oscar Robertson in Cincinnati. Playing 20 to 25 minutes a game while spelling Reed and DeBusschere, Lucas averaged 10 points, 7 rebounds, and a remarkable 4.5 assists to give New York one of the most productive sixth men in history.

In 1971–72, Los Angeles finally put it all together and won the championship. New coach Bill Sharman came in and, as was his habit, got the veteran team into excellent condition. Chamberlain was told to forget about scoring and just concentrate on dominating the paint, while West and Goodrich were instructed to shoot and let Wilt and Happy Hairston handle the rebounding. Elgin Baylor's knees gave out early in the year but his replacement, Jim McMillian, provided the jump shooting and driving the Lakers needed to keep opposing forwards occupied. Meanwhile, Pat Riley, Leroy Ellis, John Trapp, and Flynn Robinson provided experienced help off the bench. The formula proved almost unbeatable. In fact, from early November to early January, the Lakers *were* unbeatable, winning 33 games in a row. By season's end, the team had even surpassed the 76er record of 68 wins, winning a total of 69. In the playoffs, Los Angeles polished off the Bulls, Bucks, and Knicks while barely breaking a sweat.

Floor leader Walt Frazier was the glue that held together the championship New York Knicks teams of 1969–70 and 1972–73.

sists, and as the numbers suggest he was a nightmare to guard. Archibald could pop jumpers all night from 20 to 25 feet, but when defenders came out to get him, he used an explosive first step to go right down the middle, drawing countless fouls and racking up hundreds of assists.

The only player more fun to watch in the open court was Murphy, who played his entire career with the Rockets. A 5'9" water bug who skittered around the court with amazing speed, he was the league's supreme pest both on offense and defense. Underappreciated in his time, Murphy kept a mediocre Houston team from slipping too far below .500 during the early 1970s, and proved the perfect complement to Moses Malone in the late 1970s, when the team was a perennial contender. As for White, he also was an excellent complementary player, running the Celtic offense with passion and intelligence for most of the decade. He rarely took a bad shot, and never let an opponent beat him with the same move twice. The Celtics had some superb players, but without White, it is hard to imagine Boston as a serious contender during the 1970s.

Among the other notable NBA stars of the 1970s were a group of flashy, high-scoring players led by Pete Maravich, Bob McAdoo, Spencer Haywood, Gail Goodrich, and Charlie Scott. Each man was viewed as somewhat "flawed" while he played—either because his game lacked dimension, or because his team was not a perennial contender. Still, they struck fear into the hearts of opponents every time they set foot on a basketball court. Maravich was a classic example. When he came out of college in 1970 he joined an Atlanta Hawks team that already had three established scorers in Walt Hazzard, Lou Hudson, and Walt Bellamy. The chemistry was never there, and eventually the Hawks started marketing themselves as the Pistol Pete Show, which of course gave the team almost no chance of winning. Maravich was later traded to the New Orleans Jazz, where it was basically the same story. One of the most heated debates among historians is how his career might have been different had he landed in a different situation. By all accounts, Maravich was ready, willing, and able to contribute to a winning team effort.

Life After Wooden

The post-Wooden years in college basketball saw the rise to prominence of several programs that had long been dormant. Much debate surrounded which school would replace UCLA as the dominant postseason competitor, but that was because no one could remember a time when there was not a dominant team. As it turned out, no single school gained a stranglehold on the top spot in the national polls, much less the NCAA Tournament.

Indiana University was the first school to establish itself. Coached by hot-tempered Bobby Knight, the Hoosiers rolled to a 32–0 record in 1975–76 and wiped out the University of Michigan 86-68 in the NCAA final. Marquette University, one of the consistently good teams throughout the 1970s, took the 1977 NCAA crown behind the coaching of Al McGuire and the steady play of Jerome Whitehead, Bo Ellis, and Butch Lee. Ironically, the Warriors came into the tournament off their worst season in 10 years, but played solid ball to make McGuire's last game as a coach a memorable one. Kentucky, with its usual big, disciplined team, took the 1978 championship.

This burst of new college champions was accompanied by a burst of new fans. But it was the 1978–79 campaign that put college basketball on an altogether new level. That season two very popular players led previously unheralded teams to a showdown in the NCAA final. Larry Bird, who played forward, center, and guard for Indiana State University, led his team to a 29–0 record entering the tournament. Earvin Johnson, the tallest point guard anyone had ever seen, led Michigan State University into the NCAAs with a 21–6 mark. Together, they would make history.

Fiery coach Bobby Knight and player-of-the-year Scott May led the Indiana Hoosiers to a perfect 32–0 season and a national championship in 1975–76.

Bird, an Indiana native, averaged 30 points and 20 rebounds as a high-school senior, and accepted a scholarship from Bobby Knight to play for Indiana. College life did not agree with the small-town kid, so he left school, got married, worked as a garbage collector, and then got divorced. Suddenly, college life did not seem so bad. Bird accepted a scholarship at smaller Indiana State and, after sitting out a year, he averaged over 30 points a game in 1976–77 and again in 1977–78. The Boston Celtics drafted him in 1978 as a junior, but he decided to stay in school. It was a wise decision, for he led the Sycamores to an undefeated regular season and was voted college Player of the Year. Bird could shoot from anywhere on the floor, even with a couple of defenders hanging on him. The reason the team was so good was that Bird was an extraordinary passer—when defenses collapsed on him he was a wizard at finding the open man.

Johnson, who literally grew up dribbling a basketball around the streets of Lansing, stayed in town to become the star of the Michigan State Spartans. Johnson developed his ballhandling skills believing he would always play point guard, but by the time he reached college he stood 6'9". Rather than switch to forward, he stayed at the point position and revolutionized the game. Johnson's size was a tremendous advantage—he could see the entire court over his defender, and was able to post up smaller opponents. As a freshman, "Magic" led the Spartans to a 25–5 record and developed a terrific on-court relationship with high-flying forward Greg Kelser. In his sophomore year, Johnson became the most charismatic leader in college basketball, and he led the Spartans to a share of the 1979 Big Ten title. Four easy wins in the NCAA Tournament set up the showdown with Bird.

The two All-Americans elevated the NCAA final to major-event status that evening. More than 38 percent of the televisions in use in the United States were tuned to the Michigan State–Indiana State game, and the total viewing audience Bird and Magic drew was larger than any basketball audience in history—pro or college. Johnson scored a game-high 24 points and the swarming Spartan defense held Bird to just 19 as Michigan State won 75-64. What really mattered, though, was that the world had caught on to college basketball in a big way. And as it happened, at the very same time interest in pro basketball had been on the wane. The 1979 NCAA final brought enduring fame to a couple of lightly regarded colleges and turned a couple of college kids into highly marketable folk heroes. This kind of star power instantly attracted new advertisers and sponsors to college basketball, bringing more attention and money to the sport than anyone had ever thought possible. This trend would grow to astounding levels during the 1980s, making college hoops America's hottest winter sport.

Larry Bird is hemmed in by Magic Johnson (left) and Jay Vincent (right) during Michigan State's victory over Indiana State in the 1979 NCAA final. This first meeting between Bird and Johnson generated phenomenal excitement, as would their battles in the NBA playoffs.

After the Merger

When the ABA succumbed after its 1975–76 season, the National Basketball Association was again the only game in town. As expected, the incoming players had a dramatic effect on the balance of power. In the Eastern Division, Julius Erving was sold by the Nets to the Philadelphia 76ers in order to pay off the $7 million debt incurred when the team bought into the NBA. Erving joined a team starring ABA alumnus George McGinnis and Doug Collins, a big guard with an excellent shot. Among the other notable Sixers were ABA refugee Caldwell Jones, and a trio of stylish but undisciplined youngsters named Darryl Dawkins, Lloyd Free, and Joe Bryant. The loaded Sixers ran away with the division in 1976–77. In the NBA's Central Division, guard John Lucas and center Moses Malone came over from the ABA and transformed the Houston Rockets into an awesome team. The Denver Nuggets joined the league's Midwest Division and promptly became its best team, with David Thompson and Dan Issel pouring in nearly 50 points a game and defensive wizard Bobby Jones shutting down the league's top scoring forwards.

In the Pacific Division, ABA enforcer Maurice Lucas joined the Portland Trailblazers, where coach Jack Ramsay had junked starters Sidney Wicks, Lloyd Neal, and Geoff Petrie, and promoted hard-working Bob Gross and Dave Twardzik to the starting lineup. With guards Lionel Hollins and rookie Johnny Davis hustling the ball down the court, center Bill Walton found himself in the middle of a team that was eerily reminiscent of his old UCLA squad. In other words, the Blazers were built specifically to take advantage of his talents. It took a while for this new bunch to mesh, but they finished the season strong, just four games behind Kareem Abdul-Jabbar and the Lakers. The 76ers rolled through the playoffs, beating Boston and Houston in tough series. Portland had it a little easier, defeating the Bulls in the new best-of-three first round, then disposing of the Nuggets and Lakers.

Julius Erving was at his spectacular best in his first NBA All-Star Game, spinning and slamming his way to 30 points and the 1977 game's MVP trophy.

In the finals, Philadelphia's superstars—even with the Doctor's scintillating play—could not solve the unselfish, heads-up play of the Blazers. Walton shot, passed, and rebounded as well as any center in history. Lucas banged the boards and scored big buckets, and Hollins rarely made a bad decision bringing the ball down the court. What won it in the end for Portland, however, was the all-out defense Gross played on Erving, and the stunning play of Davis, who gave the 76er guards all they could handle at both ends of the court. The remarkable victory had everyone talking dynasty—the Blazers were a young, well-coached team with a star who was willing to share the spotlight. Sadly, it was not to be. The next season, the team's record stood at 50–10 when Walton broke his foot and missed the rest of the year. Gross snapped his ankle a few games later. Not only did this end Portland's season, but neither man ever recovered fully and the Blazers ended up as little more than an intriguing footnote in NBA history.

The sudden demise of the Blazers created a power vacuum in the NBA. It was filled by the Seattle Supersonics, who had enjoyed mild success when Bill Russell coached them in the mid-1970s, but had never really scared anyone. After a 5–17 start, Lenny Wilkens was hired and the new coach turned the team around; the Sonics

Though chronic injuries cut short his career, Bill Walton brought Bill Russell to mind with his rebounding and shot-blocking, and he was a marvelous passer. Here he contests a Julius Erving layup in the 1977 NBA Finals.

went 42–18 the rest of the way. Seattle had young centers Marvin Webster and Jack Sikma on a front line with veterans Paul Silas and John Johnson. In the backcourt, the team started Dennis Johnson, a smart, physical player, along with a couple of streak shooters, Gus Williams and "Downtown" Freddy Brown. Aside from Silas and Wilkens, most fans were unfamiliar with this group as they headed into the 1978 postseason. That changed when they squeezed past the Lakers, Blazers, and Nuggets in the playoffs and nearly knocked off the Bullets, who had added veteran Bob Dandridge to the All-Star frontcourt of Elvin Hayes and Wes Unseld. These two teams met again in the 1979 finals, and Seattle killed the Bullets 4–1. It marked the first time since 1951 that a team without an identifiable superstar had managed to win the NBA championship.

College Ball in the 1980s

In 1967, the NCAA—in an ill-advised attempt to impede the evolution of basketball—outlawed the slam dunk. Many coaches felt the dunk shot gave an advantage to black players; Lew Alcindor was often the example cited—his sky-hook was good enough; add the dunk and he'd score 50 points a game. When the NCAA realized it had to allow the best players to use their best moves, they allowed the dunk back into the game during the 1970s, and the play became increasingly popular. By decade's end, Julius Erving and David Thompson had raised it to an electrifying art form, and soon every high-school kid with any leaping ability was practicing his dunking style. By the late 1970s, players had taken a cue from Darryl Dawkins of the 76ers and were beginning to name their dunks. They were even giving themselves and their teams funky nicknames. In 1980, the University of Louisville became the first dunk-crazy college to make the NCAA finals, and the media just loved the high-flying fast-talking Cardinals. The team was led by Darrell "Dr. Dunkenstein" Griffith, a 6'4" guard who could leap high and hang in the air. His cohorts called themselves the

"Doctors of Dunk". Griffith made good on his guarantee to bring an NCAA title to Louisville, as the Cards scored a wild comeback victory against UCLA in the championship game.

The NCAA dunkfest had to wait a year while Indiana rolled to the NCAA title behind the astonishing play of sophomore point guard Isiah Thomas. In the 1981 tournament final the Hoosiers beat favored North Carolina, as Thomas took control on offense in the second half, and the Tar Heel frontcourt of Sam Perkins, James Worthy, and Al Wood was shut down over the final 20 minutes. Indiana Coach Bobby Knight, who earlier had proclaimed his team the "worst hand of cards" in his career, took an easy 63-50 victory from Dean Smith.

As expected, Smith returned to the NCAA final with Perkins and Worthy in 1982, but this time he was the one with the ace up his sleeve. A freshman guard had made the Tar Heel starting lineup that year, but this was no ordinary freshman. Although his numbers (13.4 points and 4.4 rebounds per game) were modest, Michael Jordan's skills were not. The 6'6" Jordan played beautifully within UNC's conservative offense, breaking down defenses with his dribble, making good decisions on the perimeter, and hitting more than half his shots from the field. And every so often, Jordan would rise majestically toward the basket and stuff the ball. His dunks were not fancy or particularly thunderous—nothing at all like the rim-rocking jams other college stars were trying—but he did seem to hang in the air for an unnatural length of time. Still, when Carolina squared off against Georgetown University in the 1982 NCAA final, Jordan was barely mentioned during the pregame buildup.

Most of the attention was focused on Georgetown's John Thompson, the first black coach to guide a team to the finals. A backup to Bill Russell during his brief pro career, Thompson was a big believer in defense and an excellent motivator. He had a Russell-like center in freshman Patrick Ewing and a group of tough and talented players including guard Sleepy Floyd. The 1982 final played out as advertised, with Ewing dominating inside for Georgetown and Worthy pouring in points for Carolina in a riveting seesaw battle. With 25 seconds left and his team down by a point, coach Smith called a play for Jordan. The freshman drifted across the court while the Hoyas

Isiah Thomas, a 6'1" dynamo, burst onto the college basketball scene in 1979–80. As a sophomore he led Indiana to an NCAA championship, then opted for the NBA over more of Bobby Knight's browbeating coaching style.

kept their eyes on Worthy and Perkins, took a pass from point guard Jimmy Black and calmly banked in a 16-footer for the game-winning basket. The next day Jordan saw his name in the basketball headlines for the first time. It would not be the last.

Jordan expanded his repertoire during the 1982–83 season to include some of the eye-popping dunks that would become his trademark, and he won his first of two straight NCAA Player of the Year trophies. But the school that really made a name for itself during 1983 and 1984 was the University of Houston. Guy Lewis, who coached Elvin Hayes in the 1960s, had himself another excellent center in Akeem Olajuwon (Olajuwon's first name would later become Hakeem). He also had Clyde Drexler and Larry Michaux, a pair of forwards who lived to throw the ball down. Coach Lewis encouraged his team to dunk the ball whenever possible, and soon the Cougars were known as "Phi Slama Jama". Houston ran its opponents off the court all season long, but ran into trouble in the NCAA final, when North Carolina State University coach Jim Valvano devised a slow-down strategy that kept the game close. In the final moments, Wolfpack forward Lorenzo Charles converted an air ball into a buzzer-beating dunk to pull off one of the biggest upsets in tournament history. Houston returned to the championship game in 1984 to face John Thompson's Hoyas in a game billed as a nuclear war between Ewing and Olajuwon. That confrontation proved to be a dud, as both players spent the game in foul trouble. Meanwhile, the Houston extras were no match for their Georgetown counterparts, including point guard Mark Jackson and swingmen David Wingate and Reggie Williams. The final score was 84-75.

As Dean Smith and the North Carolina bench explode into celebration, freshman Michael Jordan (23) glides back down court after hitting the game-winning jumper in the 1982 NCAA final. It was the first of many daggers Jordan would stick into the heart of an opponent during his storied basketball career.

Ewing and Olajuwon were the two premiere college centers in the years following the breakup of the UCLA dynasty, but they did have two noteworthy contemporaries. Ralph Sampson of the University of Virginia and Sam Perkins of North Carolina brought something crucial to the center position: mobility. While Ewing and Olajuwon were classic, post-up players in college, Sampson and Perkins could do a lot of other things. Sampson, at 7'4", was graceful, agile, and quick. He could put the ball on the floor, finish the break, and even pull up and pop a quick jumper. No one had much luck guarding him during his college career, and he was regarded by many as the most exciting player in all of basketball—college or pro—during his last three seasons with the Cavaliers. Perkins, who stood 6'10", was even more versatile. He had a collection of quick, strong inside moves as well as excellent shooting range that extended past 20 feet. Sometimes, the Tar Heels brought the ball down the court and waited for Perkins to establish position in the paint. At other times, he would pop out to the perimeter and handle the ball like a guard. His versatility opened up countless opportunities for teammates Jordan and Worthy.

The top college forwards of the late 1970s and early 1980s included a quartet of excellent scorers: Adrian Dantley, Marques Johnson, Mark Aguirre, and Wayman Tisdale. Dantley and Aguirre brought to the court a lethal combination of pure shooting skill and rugged physical strength, with "A.D." winning NCAA Player of the Year honors for Notre Dame in 1976 and Aguirre doing the same as a sophomore with DePaul in 1980. Johnson, a sophomore member of UCLA's 1975 championship squad, became the star of the Bruins and was voted the nation's top player in 1977. Though not as beefy as Dantley and Aguirre, he was just as good around the basket, with quick moves, an accurate short-range jumper, and an uncanny ability to come up with key rebounds. Tisdale, who starred for Oklahoma University a few years later, brought together the best aspects of these three players. A magnificent physical specimen with all the offensive moves, shooting talent, and rebounding skill, he averaged between 24 and 27 points a game for the Sooners and earned first-team All-America honors in each of his three college seasons.

High-altitude play: Georgetown's Patrick Ewing shoots over Houston's Akeem Olajuwon during the 1984 NCAA final.

The guard position was rich, too, during this era, although few players besides Jordan dominated play as Phil Ford, Danny Ainge, and Chris Mullin did. Ford, who led the UNC Tar Heels in the late 1970s, was the top player in the nation for 1978. He ran Dean Smith's offense better than anyone before or since, combining quickness, intelligence and a deadly scoring touch. Ainge, who played baseball for the Toronto Blue Jays during the summer, spent his winters making the world take notice of Brigham Young University's basketball program. At 6'5", he was one of the first big guards to enter college with a fully developed set of offensive skills. His ballhandling and aggressive defense were the glue of the BYU team, but he also knew when to take control and become a one-man show. The 1981 Player of the Year, Ainge averaged 24.4 points a game as a senior, and played virtually every minute of every game. Mullin, who won Player of the Year honors as a St. John's senior in 1985, led a team that included three other Big East stars: forward Walter Berry, center Bill Wennington, and guard Mark Jackson. At 6'7" Mullin picked up where Ainge left off, becoming the best big guard in college. He could shoot, dribble, and pass, and he was as good as anyone at finishing plays.

Big Changes

The 1984 NCAA final between Olajuwon's Cougars and Ewing's Hoyas marked the last time two big-time centers faced each other with a national championship on the line. In an indirect way, this was the fault of the NCAA. College basketball was surging in popularity, but there was one trend that a lot of the games decision-makers found troubling: For a decade, scoring had been steadily declining. Although the game and the athletes had evolved remarkably, good defense still beat good offense. And with better athletes available, coaches were able to come up with super-tough defenses. Against such set-ups, it took a little longer to work the ball for a good shot, and that was eating up time on the clock. So even though shooting was improving, teams just were not putting as many points on the board. The solution was to introduce the 45-second shot clock to college basketball. NCAA officials knew it might lower the quality of shots taken, but the bottom line was that more shots would translate into more points. And the public seemed to want more points.

The effect this rule had on the center position was disastrous. Against a good zone defense, it can take a long time to work the ball into the center. He must establish position, double-teaming defenders must be drawn away, and then a safe entry pass must be made. Furthermore, a good center is expected to kick the ball back out if he does not have the shot he wants. A team might start the whole process all over again, hoping it works the next time. This back-and-forth pattern was a staple of college basketball for 70 years, although no one seemed to recognize this important fact when the shot clock was introduced. In the ensuing years, teams spent less time working the ball inside and more time driving and shooting from outside. When the three-point line became a part of the college game, there was almost no reason to set up plays for the center. Over the next dozen years, the only successful offensive centers were the rare ones who could run the court, like David Robinson, or shoot from outside, like Christian Laettner.

Another change in the college game during the early 1980s was the banding together of schools and the creation of new conferences. At the root of this development was television. It was much easier for an entire conference to negotiate a lucrative television contract than it was for individual schools. And it was in the interest of individual schools to get television coverage—not just for the revenues, but to recruit top high-school players who wanted the national TV exposure. The most important new conference was the Big East, which brought together top programs such as Georgetown, St. John's, and Villanova University. The Big East was an instant success, as the 1985 NCAA final proved. Georgetown, playing for the championship for the third time in four years, fell to Villanova in a beautifully played contest. The Hoyas reached the final by defeating St. John's, meaning three of the schools in the Final Four hailed from the Big East. In all, 10 new Division-I leagues formed between 1980 and 1983, and several top independent teams joined established conferences.

Bird, Magic, and a Brand-New Era

The rise of the unheralded Sonics in the late 1970s was heralded by some as the dawn of a new era in the NBA—a triumph of sorts for the sport of basketball. When a team without a marquee-caliber go-to guy could maneuver its way to the championship, it meant that team play ultimately would win over big-name stars. Dr. Naismith himself would have applauded this development! But there were a couple of problems with this thinking. First, the alternative explanation was that the NBA had become so dominated by one-on-one stylists looking to put up big numbers and attain superstar status that no one but the Sonics was playing consistent team ball—not a triumph, but a tragedy. Second, it was nice to see a team of "foot soldiers" succeed, but this did not pull fans into NBA arenas. Team play *was* beautiful, but the fans wanted to see it executed by the generals, the emperors, the superstars.

At the end of the 1970s, in fact, pro basketball was not flourishing, it was in desperate trouble. The charismatic stars of the 1970s—Abdul-Jabbar, Maravich, Cowens, Frazier, Archibald—were on the wane. There were talented scorers around like David Thompson, George Gervin, Bob McAdoo, and Lloyd "World B." Free, but for the most part they were one-dimensional gunners who seemed only marginally interested in winning. In fact, outside of the spectacular and always-classy Dr. J, it was not entirely clear who among the younger players in the league would carry the banner for the league and captivate the fans. Attendance for many franchises was going down instead of up, and the television networks were losing interest, too. In 1980, the NBA Finals were actually shown on tape delay in many parts of the U.S! All but seven franchises were losing money, and at least five were teetering on the edge of bankruptcy.

Feeding this climate of disenchantment were rumors that many of the NBA's best players were habitual drug users. David Thompson would see his career ruined by cocaine, and a major newspaper reported that three of every four NBA players used drugs. Also, at the end of the 1970s, the NBA's three most important markets—New York, Los Angeles, and Boston—had boring teams. The Knicks were attempting to play team ball without any team players, Abdul-Jabbar of the Lakers had clearly lost interest in basketball, and the Celtics had become a team of castoffs and malcontents. Perhaps the best gauge of basketball's dire situation is that, when the Boston franchise was offered for sale for a measly $20 million, there were no takers for pro basketball's most fabled team.

The Knicks would struggle through most of the 1980s, but the Celtics and Lakers made sudden and miraculous recoveries. And this gave the NBA a shot in the arm it desperately needed. Boston took Indiana

State forward Larry Bird, then a junior, with the sixth pick in the 1978 draft; it was a gamble, as Bird fully intended to play his last year at Indiana State and if the Celtics failed to sign him before the 1979 draft, they would lose their rights to him. After a nail-biting negotiation, the Celtics brought Bird into the fold with only a week to spare, signing him to what was at that time the largest contract ever awarded a rookie in any sport.

A one-man show in college, Bird fit beautifully into the Celtic team concept and immediately made everyone around him better. His outside shooting stretched enemy defenses and enabled aging veterans Dave Cowens and Nate Archibald to drive to the basket. It also gave power forward Cedric Maxwell more room to maneuver inside, and he ended up shooting 61 percent for the season. Off-guard Chris Ford worked the other side of the perimeter, so if defenses shifted to stop Bird, a second outside shooter was available at all times. Bird averaged 21 points and 10 rebounds for the season, and won Rookie of the Year honors.

In 1981 Larry Bird led the Boston Celtics—just two years away from the Atlantic Division cellar—to the team's 14th NBA championship. Afterward, Bird had the audacity to swipe Red Auerbach's victory cigar—much to Auerbach's obvious delight.

In Los Angeles, the Lakers had a rookie owner, Jerry Buss, and a rookie point guard, Magic Johnson. Magic's tremendous all-around play boosted the team to the 60-win plateau, and his boundless enthusiasm ignited a spark in 32-year-old Abdul-Jabbar, who went to the basket with gusto and played better defense than he had in years. Jamaal Wilkes (who changed his name from Keith after converting to Islam) had become a potent scorer, and guard Norm Nixon had no trouble sharing the L.A. backcourt with Magic.

Johnson was quite unlike anything anyone had ever seen in the NBA. He had the ballhandling and passing skills of a six-footer, the slashing ability of a small forward, and he could play with his back to the basket, like a center. Nixon, who had been one of the leagues up-and-coming point guards, had a good enough shot to be the shooting guard when Magic ran the offense, and switched smoothly over to the point when his 20-year-old teammate decided to post up his man. A young defensive forward named Michael Cooper provided fresh legs for veterans Jim Chones and Spencer Haywood, enabling the team to run the ball right down opponents' throats.

The Lakers took on the defending-champion Sonics in the conference finals and destroyed them, then went up against the 76ers in the NBA Finals. Philadelphia had strengthened itself with the acquisitions of guard Lionel Hollins, forward Bobby Jones, and center Caldwell Jones, while the development of home-grown stars Darryl Dawkins and Maurice Cheeks made the Sixers all the more dangerous. Abdul-Jabbar, sensing this might be his last shot at a title, played beautifully in the series and helped the Lakers gain a 3–2 advantage. But in the fifth game he severely sprained his ankle, and could not go the rest of the way. Without a center to deal with Dawkins and Jones, the Lakers seemed doomed.

To the rescue came Magic Johnson, who shifted from point guard to center for Game 6 in Philadelphia and put on the most astonishing show in playoff history. He shut down Phillys' big men with his quick feet and hands, and then beat them down the court time and again for easy scores. With the Sixers watching in total disbelief, Los Angeles won 123-107 behind "big man" Magic, who scored 42 points and collected 15 rebounds.

A few days later, the Celtics pulled off a major coup. A season earlier they had acquired Detroit's top pick for veteran Bob McAdoo. The Pistons finished 16–66, which meant that the Celtics owned the number-one pick in the 1980 draft. With Cowens ready to retire, everyone assumed the Celts would take Purdue University center Joe Barry Carroll. But general manager Red Auerbach dealt the Detroit pick to the Golden State Warriors in exchange for the third overall pick in the draft and a skinny young center named Robert Parish, who Golden State would no longer need after drafting Carroll. The Celtics then took University of Minnesota forward Kevin McHale. Both Parish and McHale fit into the Boston offense perfectly, combining with Maxwell to produce 45 points and 20 rebounds a game from the center and power forward positions. With Bird leading the way, the Celtics rolled straight to the finals in 1981, where they beat Moses Malone and the Houston Rockets.

The NBA was still having problems, but with Bird and Johnson it had two shining examples of what the game should and could be. They had different styles, but both made all their teammates better, and both played to win. Most important, each young star already had a championship under his belt. All that remained was a showdown in

Moses Malone bulls his way to the basket. The Sixers added Malone—a two-time MVP and the league's best rebounder—prior to the 1982–83 season, then rang up a 65–17 regular-season record and breezed through the playoffs to a title.

A STEADY HAND

Though 1982–83 was hailed as the year of the Sixers, it was an important one for the NBA as a whole. The league made a television deal with ESPN to broadcast weekly games on cable, and came to a similar agreement with the USA network for the following season. The NBA's move onto cable would generate millions in revenue, and bring the game to millions of viewers whose primary exposure to the NBA had been CBS's playoff broadcasts each spring.

These deals were initiated by David Stern, who had joined the NBA in 1978 and was in charge of public relations, marketing, and broadcasting. Later in 1983, he was named league commissioner. Stern inherited control of a sport that could have gone in one of two directions. The NBA was suffering through a period of shrinking attendance and bad publicity. On the court, however, pro basketball was being played with great style and exuberance.

Stern, who had helped to develop the league's licensing, merchandising, video, and publishing arms, turned to these divisions and instructed them to grow the game. The NBA reached out to kids, women, and fans of other sports as never before, and within a few years the league had righted itself. Television continued to play a major role in the revitalization plan, as did the focus placed on basketball's young stars, including Michael Jordan, Patrick Ewing, and Charles Barkley. Stern also brought NBA telecasts to dozens of overseas markets, and within a few years a steady flow of top European talent began. Among the commissioner's other important contributions was a tough but fair antidrug policy, and an agreement with the players that gave them a guaranteed share of the NBA's revenue while creating a salary cap under which owners could operate. David Stern pushed the game's strengths and shored up its weaknesses, and it is hard to imagine where the league would be without him.

the NBA Finals, but that would not come until 1984. In the meantime, it was the perennially talented but underachieving 76ers' turn to hoist a championship banner over their floor.

In the years following the NBA-ABA merger, Philadelphia seemed to hold all the cards. Besides the miraculous Dr. J, they had size, strength, speed, and scoring, plus a constant flow of young talent. What kept them from winning it all, however, was their lack of a consistent center. Caldwell Jones was a good defender and rebounder, but he contributed nothing on offense. Darryl Dawkins had matured into a potent offensive force, but he was not a dependable defender. When Moses Malone became a free agent in the summer of 1983, the 76ers grabbed him and got rid of Dawkins and Jones. In 1982–83 they rolled to 65 wins and Malone won his second consecutive MVP award. Everyone predicted the 76ers would sweep every series on their way to the NBA championship, and they nearly did, dropping just one game to the Bucks in the conference finals. Not even Magic and Kareem could hold off the Philadelphia onslaught, as the Sixers swept the Lakers out of the finals in four games.

The anticipated showdown of Bird and Johnson in the NBA finals finally came to be in the spring of 1984. It was an exciting series, during which the Lakers had every chance to win but could not close the deal. In the first four games they scored two blowouts against the Celtics, but dropped a pair of overtime decisions to leave the door open for Bird and company. The teams split Games 5 and 6 to send the series back to the Boston Garden for Game 7. There Cedric Maxwell took control of the action, punishing the Lakers inside and making a key steal in the game's waning moments. The series was as good as advertised, with Johnson and Bird involved at all times, and both men exhibiting their considerable skills. Bird got the best of this battle, averaging 27 points and 14 rebounds, but the most important numbers were the TV ratings for Game 7: the contest had drawn more television viewers than any game in NBA history. In just a few years the league had come back from the brink of disaster and was entering its most prosperous era.

A few days later, that era would start officially when the Chicago Bulls selected Michael Jordan with the third pick in the NBA draft. No one knew it at the time, but the league had just found the perfect young player to take it to the next level. With Bird and Johnson established as the ultimate team-concept players, what the NBA needed was a showman who could carry the

There was almost no defense against Magic Johnson—at a muscular 6'9" with point-guard skills, he could haul in a rebound, push the ball down the floor himself, and either take it to the hoop or deliver one of his patented no-look passes for a dunk.

torch Julius Erving would soon be passing on. Jordan had been named college Player of the Year that spring, but because he played in Dean Smith's conservative offense, few NBA fans were aware of what an immense talent he was. As the Lakers and Celtics raced toward another meeting in the 1986 NBA Finals, Jordan quietly put together a monster season for the Bulls and began doing things on the basketball court that no one had ever seen before.

Although Jordan sparked a 10-game improvement with his fabulous rookie season in 1984–85, the Bulls were still years away from contending. The powerhouse franchises were still the Lakers and Celtics. By the mid-1980s, Los Angeles had assembled quite a team. Under coach Pat Riley the Lakers, stacked with great athletes, ran opponents off the court with an otherworldly fast-break offense. "Showtime" had an exuberant leader in Magic, whose unique ability to rebound, push the ball coast-to-coast, and either pass or take it in himself led to layup after layup for the Lakers. The team was solid from top to bottom. Athletic jump-shooter Byron Scott replaced Nixon at the off-guard. At forward, Los Angeles had James Worthy, an explosive 6'9" performer who was lethal both on the break and in the halfcourt, where he shot with tremendous accuracy. In the power forward slot was Kurt Rambis, whose Clark Kent glasses masked a smart and scrappy competitor. And Kareem was still good for three quarters a night if the team needed him. Backing up the Laker starting five were swingman Michael Cooper, who had added a deadly three-pointer to his arsenal, and power forward A.C. Green, who eventually replaced Rambis in the starting lineup. Between 1984–85 and 1987–88, the Los Angeles Lakers won three NBA championships, establishing themselves as the "Team of the Eighties."

The Celtics and their fans, of course, disputed the Lakers claim to this title. The Celts topped the 60-win mark six times in the 1980s, peaking under coach K.C. Jones in the middle of the decade. Bird scored, rebounded, and passed his way to three

Larry Bird, the NBA's Most Valuable Player for three straight years in the mid-1980s, shoots a three-pointer late in a game against the Atlanta Hawks.

Kevin McHale tosses up a baby hook over a defender. McHale, Larry Bird, and Robert Parish formed the Big Three, the frontcourt that powered the Boston Celtics to three NBA titles in the 1980s.

straight league-MVP awards from 1983–84 through 1985–86. Like a chess grandmaster, Bird always seemed to be way ahead of other players in seeing how a play could develop, and his court sense and killer playmaking instinct were the heart and soul of the Boston attack. Meanwhile, Parish had developed into a durable center who could put the ball in the basket from a number of spots on the floor. McHale, with impossibly long arms and an endless bag of moves, had become one of the finest post players in the game, and a perfect complement for Bird and Parish. The guard situation, which had held the team back earlier in the decade, had resolved itself with former Sonic Dennis Johnson and college star Danny Ainge sharing the load. The Celtics could not stop Showtime in 1985 when they again met the Lakers in the finals, but 1986 would be a different story. Bill Walton returned from the dead to play a critical backup role and the Celtics dominated the league, rolling up 67 wins and taking their third championship banner of the decade with a 4–2 win in the finals over the Houston Rockets.

The Celtics and Lakers clashed one more time in the postseason, with L.A. taking a 4–2 decision from an injury-riddled, exhausted, but still dangerous Boston team. It was a classic series decided in the waning moments of Game 4 when Magic gave the Lakers a 3–1 lead by hitting a "junior, junior, junior sky hook" over the outstretched arms of Bird, Parish, and McHale.

Stars of the 1980s

There was more to the NBA during the Celtic-Laker years than just the Celtics and Lakers. On the bad side, the drug problem continued to spread. Some players were caught and punished, while others avoided detection and just watched their careers go down the drain. Drugs, in fact, spelled the end of any hope for a new Celtic dynasty when the team's top 1986 draft pick, Len Bias, died of a cocaine overdose the day after he was selected. On the good side, there were a number of charismatic young players entering the league, as well as a few magnificent veterans.

For most of the late 1970s and 1980s, Kareem Abdul-Jabbar and Moses Malone dominated the center position. They approached their position very differently. As he had when he first broke into the league, Abdul-Jabbar used his marvelous athleticism and finesse to put points on the board. His sky hook remained an unstoppable weapon, he was a great passer out of the post, and although he faded a bit on defense and around the backboards as he aged he still ranked among the league's top big men in these areas. Malone was an altogether different player. He used brute strength, intimidation, and a sixth sense for pulling in loose balls to win three MVP awards and take both the Rockets and 76ers to the NBA Finals. Though he stood just 6'10", Malone dominated every center of his era, especially in the paint, where he established himself as history's most talented offensive rebounder. This actually was a skill he possessed back when he broke into the ABA as a teenager, and he developed it further in practice by noticing where his teammates' misses tended to go from different spots on the floor.

Forty-year-old Kareem Abdul-Jabbar launches a sky-hook during the 1988 NBA Finals. He finished his career with six championship rings, six MVP awards, and a record-smashing 38,387 points.

Aside from these two giants there was not much in the way of multitalented big men until Patrick Ewing and Hakeem Olajuwon came out of college—and their biggest impact would not come until the 1990s. Ralph Sampson, the University of Virginia star, had a brief shining moment for the Houston Rockets, but knee problems cut him down. Had he remained healthy, gained some weight, and continued to develop his game, there is no telling what he might have accomplished as a pro. Sampson possessed abilities that no man his size had ever displayed, but was just too fragile to hold up under the NBA's grueling 82-game schedule.

In a way, the same could be said of David Thompson. Rich, famous NBA stars are offered every kind of temptation over each long season, and Thompson's promising career was undone not by weak knees but by a weakness for cocaine. As he had in college and the ABA he was able to score virtually at will in the NBA. Thompson, who got the nickname "Skywalker" after *Star Wars* was released in 1977, had a four-foot vertical leap and he used this ability to the fullest, raining down eye-popping dunks on helpless opponents. An excellent outside shooter, Thompson was one of those rare players—like Elgin Baylor, Wilt Chamberlain, Oscar Robertson, Connie Hawkins, Pete Maravich, Julius Erving, and Michael Jordan—who could get a clean look at the basket any time he pleased. He averaged 25 points a game in his prime, mixing long-distance shooting with spectacular drives to the basket.

Among Thompson's main competition during those years was 6'7" George Gervin of the San Antonio Spurs. Like Thompson, he could play either guard or forward, but the "Ice Man" got his points in more conventional fashion, with jumpers, scoops, and a patented finger roll which drove defenders crazy. The reed-thin Gervin snaked his way to the basket as well as anyone in history, contorting his body to get off shots in heavy traffic. He had already established himself as a great shooter with the Squires and Spurs in the ABA, but he found the NBA even more to his liking. Between 1976–77 and 1984–85, he averaged between 21 and 33 points a game, leading the league in scoring four times during one five-year stretch. In most seasons, Gervin hit well over half his shots from the field—an amazing stat when one considers that most NBA players would have been benched for attempting the shots he took. On the final day of the 1977–78 season, Thompson and Gervin had a legendary shootout to decide the scoring championship. Thompson went wild, piling up 71 points to pull ahead of Gervin. The Ice Man, playing in a later game, figured he needed 61 points to edge Thompson, so he went out and scored 63.

Among the more conventional guards to emerge during the Magic Johnson era were Maurice Cheeks and Sidney Moncrief.

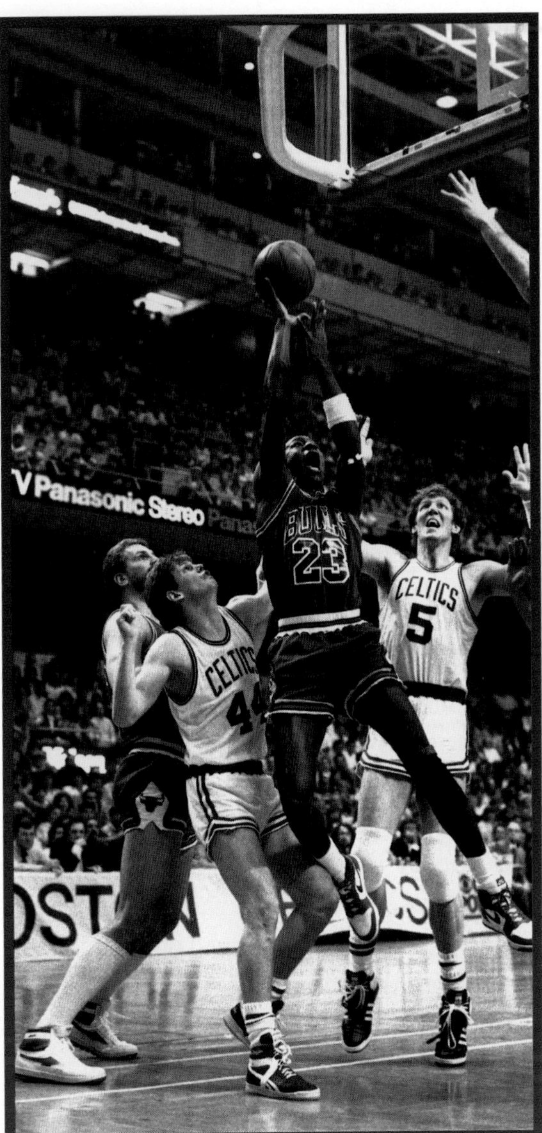

Knifing his way into a hole in the Boston defense, Michael Jordan goes for 2 of his playoff-record 63 points on April 20, 1986.

Cheeks came to the 76ers in 1978–79, which turned out to be perfect timing. Philadelphia floor general Doug Collins was hampered by a series of injuries and Henry Bibby had been a shooting guard too long to run the 76er attack. Cheeks, a virtual unknown from West Texas State University, ran the Sixer offense for the next 10 years, distributing the ball beautifully to the team's frontcourt stars and popping the occasional jumper himself. A marvelous defensive player, Cheeks could contain opposing point guards and bog down a team's offense in ways that never showed up in the statistics. His battles against the league's other top point guard, Dennis Johnson, provided basketball connoisseurs with a fascinating sidelight to the Larry Bird–Julius Erving show when the Celtics and Sixers mixed it up.

Moncrief came to the Milwaukee Bucks at approximately the same time as Cheeks, but because he had brought the University of Arkansas basketball program into national prominence as a college star, he got far more attention when he came into the NBA. Moncrief was the defensive soul of a team with high-powered offensive stars like Bob Lanier, Marques Johnson, Terry Cummings, and Rickey Pierce. A consistent 20-point scorer himself, Moncrief was an aggressive, slashing player who swooped down on opponents from the wing for twisting layups and offensive rebounds. Often, the only way to contain Moncrief was to foul him, and it was not unusual for him to make a dozen or more trips to the free throw line during a game. Though a slight notch below Bird and Magic, Moncrief was a lot closer to these two in terms of ability and leadership than most fans realized.

The most engaging guard of this period, outside of Michael Jordan, was Isiah Thomas, who left Indiana University after his sophomore year and joined the Detroit Pistons. Despite his youth, Thomas took control of the Piston offense and established a level of play that would eventually lead to an NBA championship. No other point guard during the 1980s combined ballhandling and scoring skills as well as Thomas, and Michael Jordan was the only other backcourt player who could take over a game completely for long stretches at a time. Likeable and media-smart, Thomas became one of the NBA's marquee players. It was his team that ended Boston's domination of the Eastern Conference during the late-1980s, and it would be Thomas's Pistons who would ultimately close out the Laker dynasty.

Among the forwards playing second fiddle to Larry Bird were Bernard King and Alex English. King was the kind of offensive player who could pick up a team and carry it on his back, and he did this countless times in his years with the Nets, Warriors, and Knicks. He was a great finisher on the fast break, but it was his halfcourt game that put fear into opponents. King shot the turnaround jumper with an amazingly quick release and deadly accuracy, and he worked tirelessly to perfect a handful of post moves that enabled him to get his shot off any time. He was truly unstoppable when he found the groove. English kicked around with Milwaukee and Indiana for a few years before the Pacers traded him to the Denver Nuggets (along with a first-round draft choice) for aging George McGinnis in 1980. English led the NBA in scoring in 1982–83 and averaged between 23 and 29 points a game through the 1988–89 campaign. So smooth and accurate was his shooting that few fans noticed how good he was as an offensive rebounder and shot blocker.

In 1984, the 76ers brought a unique talent and personality to the league when they drafted Charles Barkley out of Auburn University. Barkley's unusual build—6'6" and 270 pounds—and great jumping ability

A rim-rocking dunk by Charles Barkley, one of the NBA's most riveting personalities during the 1980s and 1990s.

had already earned him the nickname "Round Mound of Rebound." Barkley was vocal, physical, and highly entertaining to watch—even on a team with All-Stars Erving, Cheeks, and Malone. Within a season, Barkley was a 20-point scorer and regularly pulled down 10 to 15 rebounds a game, establishing himself as one of the league's young superstars.

With new, highly marketable players like Barkley, Jordan, Thomas, Olajuwon, and Ewing, the NBA was in great shape going into the 1990s. These players had time to develop their games and images without the intense pressure to win, because Bird and Johnson still held the spotlight. By the time these two greats began to fade, the league's next generation of stars was ready and willing to take over.

College Basketball in Fast Forward: The late 1980s and 1990s

The 1980s witnessed an era of unparalleled competition, which continued right into the 1990s. Whereas in years past only a couple of teams went into a season with a legitimate chance at winning a national championship, now as many as a dozen or more had to be considered "in the running." And with the NCAA Tournament field expanded to 64 schools in 1985, any one of a dozen more might get hot, catch a few breaks, and become national champion. From 1982 to 1991, a different school won the NCAA title each year. College basketball also began seeing an influx of foreign-born players, as the game developed rapidly at the high-school level all over the world.

In American high schools, the game was evolving faster than anyone had ever imagined possible. In the 1980s and 1990s, it became commonplace for college freshmen to play major roles in postseason competition. So good were high-school graduates that after just one season of Division-I experience they were polished and poised enough to perform like seniors. By the mid-1990s, a handful of each year's top freshmen were leaving college for the NBA. And a number of high school players, including Kevin Garnett and Kobe Bryant, jumped directly into the pros without missing a beat.

Given the number of forces at work in college basketball, it is not surprising that only one program remained consistently good throughout this period. Duke University, under coach Mike Krzyzewski, managed to put a great team on the floor almost every year. "Coach K" saw many of the changes coming, so he structured his program to get the most out of his recruiting efforts. The team's offense put a premium on intelligent, versatile players who could change the team's look each trip down the court. Each Blue Devil could play at least two positions, and much like John Wooden's old UCLA squads, Duke excelled at playing different styles of ball, as a game or opponent dictated. In order to accomplish this, Krzyzewski recruited smart, multitalented players who were willing to become part of a team rather than demand to be its focal point. He did not land the best freshmen in the country, but he did get enough good ones to make his system work. He also had to make sure his players would stick around long enough to mature in the Duke system—a player who stayed for a season or two and left hurt more than he helped. This is where the Duke atmosphere helped immeasurably. The campus was lovely, the winning tradition intoxicating, and the diploma was worth more than the paper on which it was printed; those who could have left early always chose to stay. They knew they would never have it that good again.

Duke reached the NCAA final in 1986 and advanced to the Final Four again in 1988 and 1989. In 1990, Duke returned to the final behind forward Christian Laettner and guards Bobby Hurley and Phil Henderson, but lost to a powerhouse UNLV team

Mike Krzyzewski makes an emphatic point from the sidelines during the 1988 NCAA tournament. "Coach K" and his perennially strong Duke teams have made seven Final Four appearances in the 1980s and 1990s.

led by Larry Johnson and Stacey Augmon. In 1991 the Blue Devils finally won it all, with Laettner turning in a memorable clutch performance and forward Grant Hill emerging as a special player. The team repeated as NCAA champion in 1992 (the first time in a decade that had happened), as Hill picked up the slack when their opponents collapsed around Laettner. Hill also led the Blue Devils back to the big game in 1994, after Hurley and Laettner had graduated.

The school Duke faced in the 1992 final, the University of Michigan, provided college basketball with a glimpse of things to come. Known as the "Fab Five," the Wolverines started a quintet of freshmen that season and advanced all the way to the title game. Led by guard Jalen Rose, forward Chris Webber, and center Juwan Howard, Michigan used a combination of fresh legs and in-your-face attitude to sweep past a pair of Top 10 schools in Oklahoma State and Ohio State, then beat Nick Van Exel and Cincinnati to reach the NCAA final. What the Fab Five lacked in maturity they made up for with tremendous talent and a lack of fear so complete that opponents could hardly help but be intimidated. Even the level-headed Blue Devils were a bit disarmed at first. In fact, the taunting, high-fiving Wolverines went into the locker room at halftime with a 31-30 lead. Duke's maturity and discipline won out, and Michigan's inexperience finally began to show on the foul line as the Blue Devils outscored their opponent 41-20 in the second half. Michigan's fabulous freshmen returned to the NCAA final as sophomores, but this time they ran into another impeccably coached team, Dean Smith's North Carolina Tar Heels. The game came down to the final possession, with the Wolverines needing a three-pointer to win. Carolina managed to trap Webber on the sideline with 11 seconds left. He signaled the referee for a time-out, forgetting his team had none left. The ensuing free throws made it a four-point game, and the final score was 77-71.

Chris Webber (left) and Jalen Rose, two of Michigan's talented Fab Five, talk it up during their 77-71 loss to North Carolina in the 1993 NCAA Championship game.

Although Division-I freshmen stars were becoming more plentiful, having five first-year starters was still quite a feat. Academic requirements were tightened up dramatically with the passage of Proposition

David Robinson, here blocking a William and Mary player's shot, was head and shoulders above other college centers of the late 1980s. A one-man team at Navy, he led the Midshipmen to the NCAA Regional Finals in 1986.

48, which kept high-school seniors from playing big-time basketball unless they passed a difficult college entrance examination. Charges were leveled that this discriminated against players from poor school districts, and against black players in particular. Some believed that Prop 48 denied these young men an equal right to a university education because they had the misfortune of attending a lousy high school. As the arguments raged, those who did not qualify ended up going to junior colleges, where they could get their grades up and still play basketball for one or two years before joining Division-I programs. The result of this trend was a dramatic leap in the quality of "Juco" hoops, and a lot of players joining Division-I programs as experienced, battle-hardened juniors.

Among the outstanding college players during this period were a group of forwards who shone brightly as the luster began to come off the center position. Christian Laettner was the best of the bunch, using his lanky 6'11" frame to knife into the lane and his outside shooting skill to stretch defenses for his teammates. His fashion-model looks masked a tough, nasty competitive fire that pulled Duke out of countless tight spots and contributed mightily to the school's back-to-back NCAA championships. Grant Hill, who played off of Laettner as a freshman and sophomore, blossomed in his final two years with the Blue Devils, earning first-team All-America honors in 1993 and 1994.

Danny Manning, Sean Elliott, and Larry Johnson were also All-Americans in back-to-back seasons. Manning, who earned Player of the Year honors as a senior with Kansas in 1988, was a terrific all-around player. At 6'10" he could hold his own inside, but his hallmark was his quickness and an accurate short-range jumper. In 1988, he was named the Most Outstanding Player in the NCAA Tournament as he led the Jayhawks to the national title. Elliott led the University of Arizona to a number-two ranking during the regular season in 1987–88 and took the Wildcats to the top of the polls a year later, when he was named Player of the Year. He combined good size with explosive moves to average over 19 points a game during his four years at Arizona. Johnson, a celebrated junior-college product, joined Jerry Tarkanian's UNLV Runnin' Rebels in 1989–90 and promptly led the team to the NCAA Championship. In his senior year, "L.J." was the most dominant player in the college game, averaging 22.7 points and 10.9 rebounds a contest. Johnson manhandled his opponents, posting them up, smashing into the lane for layups and tip-ins, and even firing away from three-point territory a couple of times a game.

Although the center position was going through a period of decline from the mid-1980s on, it was not totally devoid of talent. David Robinson, who grew six inches after enrolling at the U.S. Naval Academy, became one of the most exciting players in years. "The Admiral" regularly scored 25 to 30 points a game and led the nation in blocked shots and rebounds. In postseason play, Robinson was just as good, averaging 28.6 points and 12.3 rebounds in NCAA Tournament games. He was named the NCAA's top player in 1987. Shaquille O'Neal, though not as mobile and hardly as complete a player, nevertheless dominated his college opposition during three spectacular seasons at Louisiana State University. He won national Player of the Year honors in 1991, scoring 27.1 a game and leading the country in rebounding and blocked shots. An awesome physical specimen, "Shaq" made most of his points on dunks and layups. Like Robinson, he could run the floor like a forward—a key trait for the college big men of the 1990s.

During the mid-1990s only a select few players combined the size and athleticism needed to be a standout modern college center. The best were Marcus Camby and Tim Duncan. Camby, a willowy pivot man for the University of Massachusetts, could get down the floor even faster than Robinson. Though he lacked the raw power to dominate inside, he became a defensive force with his quickness and timing. On offense, he could handle the ball and shoot it as well as any center in the country—a big reason he was voted Player of the Year in 1996. While other talented players took their raw, unpolished games to the NBA after just a year or two of college, seven-footer Tim Duncan stayed at Wake Forest all the way through his senior season; it was a treat to watch him develop a complete array of post moves and solid fundamentals. A two-time All-American at Wake, Duncan joined the NBA for the 1997–98 season and proved that the patience he showed by staying in school can pay off: He wowed the league with his poised, efficient command of the game, and became the first rookie to make first-team All-NBA since Larry Bird.

Actually, if college ball is remembered for one thing during the late 1980s and 1990s it will be for the wealth of polished point guards it produced. Once the shot clock was introduced, enormous pressure was placed on college set-up men to advance the ball quickly and get the team into its offense while there was still enough time to work for a good shot. Duke's Bobby Hurley, Jason Kidd of the University of California, and Kenny Anderson and Stephon Marbury of Georgia Tech led a point-guard revolution. Most came right out of high school ready to play, and after a season or two they were NBA-caliber. Some stayed in college and some left for the pros, but there always seemed to be a half-dozen more ready to come in and take their place. Each man combined supreme quickness, dribbling, and passing skill, as well as the ability to penetrate and break down a defense. A few, like Georgetown's Allen Iverson and Arizona's Damon Stoudamire, had the scoring prowess to burn an opponent for 25 points a game. That meant they did not have to force a pass that was not there—if defenders gave them a step, they would take it and score.

By the late 1990s, the college game seemed on the verge of being dominated by these "super" point guards. The traditional set-up of a "dribbling" guard and a "shooting" guard was giving way to offensive alignments with two players who could do both, as well as a third man who could dribble and shoot at the small forward position. More and more, "playing small" produced big results, as ball movement, penetration, and outside shooting replaced post-up play. With the shot clock whittled down to 35 seconds, there is no reason to think that this trend will change significantly—at least until seven-footers begin nailing three-pointers and making behind-the-back passes on the fast break.

Dynasty in Chicago: The NBA in the 1990s

Larry, Michael, and Magic. As the 1980s melted into the 1990s, these were the words that NBA executives chanted over and over again. Bird, Jordan, and Johnson had resurrected the NBA and provided it with the three Ps: popularity, prosperity, and profitability. The team to beat, however, was not the Celtics, the Bulls, or the Lakers. It was the Detroit Pistons. In the spring of 1988, the Pistons had dumped the Celtics in the playoffs and in Game 6 of the finals came within 60 seconds of defeating the Lakers for the NBA title. While everyone was in Los Angeles was celebrating the league's first back-to-back champion since the 1960s, Detroit fans were licking their chops in anticipation of the coming season.

And with good reason. Under coach Chuck Daly, the Pistons had assembled one of the roughest and most talented squads ever. Center Bill Laimbeer could rebound, consistently hit the perimeter jumper, and was recognized as the game's preeminent cheap-shot artist on defense. Dennis Rodman, an emotional forward with a nose for trouble, quickly became an amazing offensive rebounder and the league's best one-on-one defender. At the other forward position, the Pistons played Mark Aguirre, the longtime star of the expansion Dallas Mavericks. Aguirre possessed slick moves, a tremendous scoring touch, and a tree-trunk-like lower body he used to back opponents into the basket. Also in the mix were bruiser Rick Mahorn and seven-foot shot-blocker John Salley. Isiah Thomas ran the show, but his backcourt mates were nearly as important to the team's success as he was. Joe Dumars, a highly focused and impeccably conditioned shooting guard, contributed important points from the perimeter and played awesome defense. Off the bench came one of history's most meteoric scorers, Vinnie Johnson, who was nicknamed the "Microwave" for his ability to get hot so quickly. Collectively, the Pistons were known as the "Bad Boys," and they sometimes went out of their way to cultivate this image. No one seemed able to handle them; they wore older opponents down, and drew faster teams into half-court street brawls.

The Pistons reached the NBA finals again in 1989, and demolished the Lakers. Johnson and Byron Scott were both hobbled

Detroit Pistons owner Bill Davidson and his Bad Boys celebrate their first of two consecutive NBA championships.

WOMEN'S BASKETBALL

There are a great many people who are under the impression that women's basketball is a recent phenomenon. In reality, the women's game is as old as basketball itself. Just a few weeks after Dr. James Naismith's male secretarial students first took the court at the Springfield YMCA, a group of female teachers from nearby Buckingham Grade School began watching from the balcony. Taken with his new game, the young women asked Naismith if he would show them how to play. One of the teachers, Maude Sherman, was taken with the good doctor himself, and they later married.

Women took up basketball within a few months of James Naismith's invention of the game.

From there the women's game began to spread. Sendra Berensen, the physical education director at Smith College, heard about basketball at a Yale University seminar in 1893 and spoke with Naismith about how best to modify it for women, whose movements were constricted by the traditional bloomers worn during physical activities. At Newcomb College in New Orleans, instructor Clara Baer wrote Naismith asking for a copy of the rules for his game. He obliged, and even penciled into a diagram of the court where he thought the players might be best positioned. Baer misunderstood his intentions, believing that the players had to stay in these areas. Unfortunately, she then rewrote a rulebook for women, and even renamed the women's game "Basquette." Naismith, who only wanted to see basketball grow, raised no objections to Baer's unusual spin on his game, and soon these rules were adopted by educators across the country.

Thus for the next 70 years, women's basketball adhered to a set of rules that were written by someone who did not get it. Eventually, it became a six-on-six affair, but with three players per team compelled to stay in half the court at all times —essentially making women's hoops two separate three-on-three games!

Women's basketball did manage to grow during this time, and in some areas it flourished. In Iowa, girl's basketball became wildly popular, and retained its luster there through some very lean years for the sport itself. In Canada, a commercial high school fielded a team in 1915 that grew into the most accomplished squad in North America. The Edmonton Commercial Grads toured the U.S., Canada, and eventually the world, and once won 147 consecutive games. The Grads even played men's teams from time to time, winning seven of nine contests. Eventually, the Grads developed a sophisticated "farm system" of four teams, where talent could be developed in school and at two intermediate levels before players moved up to the barnstorming team. The Grads were one of a handful of touring outfits that existed prior to World War II. These teams were viewed by many as novelty acts, but the basketball being played was quite good, and it provided excellent competition for women who wanted to play past high school and college.

The Amateur Athletic Union did what it could to encourage women's basketball. In 1926, the AAU organized a tournament in Los Angeles, and this became the focal point of the sport. In 1931, the Golden Cyclones—a team sponsored by Employers Insurance Casualty Co. in Dallas—won the title behind the wondrous skills of a teenager named Mildred "Babe" Didrikson. Later that year, she was a one-woman team at the AAU national track-and-field championships, defeating the University of Illinois (which sent 22 athletes into the fray) all by herself. Didrikson would return to L.A. a year later for the Olympics and capture the imagination of the sporting world by winning two gold medals and a silver. Didrikson was suspended by the AAU for allowing her photo to be used in an automobile advertisement, so she decided to cash in on her fame and start her own basketball team. She called it the Babe Didrikson All-Stars, and they drew large crowds as they traveled from city to city. Babe was the only woman on the team.

Cynthia Cooper, the best player of the WNBA's inaugural year, slashes to the hoop.

The AAU did not have stars to compete with Didrikson, but there were several accomplished players during this time, including Corine Jaax Smith and Alline Banks Sprouse, who earned All-America honors 20 times between them. After World War II, the dominant female player in the AAU was Nera White, a rangy six-footer who dominated women's basketball for more than 15 years. During White's reign, many of Clara Baer's ancient rules were modified or abandoned, setting the stage for the modern women's game.

In the 1970s, women's basketball got an important lift from the Association for Intercollegiate Athletics for Women, which began sponsoring national championships in 1972. During this important period, women's basketball developed its first nationally recognized superstars, including Carol Blazejowski of Montclair State, Nancy Lieberman of Old Dominion, Lucy Harris of Delta State, and Ann Meyers of UCLA. Even the most chauvinistic fan had to admit that these players could handle the ball, shoot, and play defense as well as "the guys." More important, they could draw big crowds to arenas, which suggested that pro ball was a definite possibility. Some early tries at professional leagues fell short, but the women's game never failed to learn from its mistakes and became stronger throughout the 1970s and 1980s.

In 1981, the NCAA took charge of the college game, and in the years since women's basketball has grown in popularity and quality each and every season. Lynette Woodard of Kansas, Anne Donovan of ODU, Cheryl Miller of USC, and Teresa Edwards of Georgia were the big names in the 1980s. They took control of the international game away from the USSR with Olympic gold medals in 1984 and 1988. And thanks to their pioneering efforts, in the 1990s the women's game became a big-time, money-making sport. In the spring of 1995, the NCAA final between Connecticut and Tennessee drew a television rating of 5.4—five times the rating of some of the Stanley Cup hockey games airing at the same time. Prior to this event, broadcasters were convinced that sports fans would not tune into women's team sports. The huge audience for this game began to make them think otherwise.

The true watershed year for women's ball was 1996, when the women's national team became the toast of the Olympics. After a long and highly publicized international tour Team USA rolled into Atlanta and captured a gold medal, generating enough interest among fans to spawn two professional leagues: the American Basketball League and the Women's National Basketball Association. Both circuits proved successful right away, and generated enough fan loyalty and corporate sponsorship to ensure the future of the women's pro game. And whereas a basketball expert during the 1960s would be hard-pressed to name more than one or two top players, today even the casual fan can rattle off the names of the top collegians and pros. Sheryl Swoopes, Jennifer Azzi, Lisa Leslie, Dawn Staley, Cheryl Cooper, Rebecca Lobo, Kate Starbird, Chamique Holdsclaw—these players and others are being entrusted with growing the women's game. Not just on the pro level, but from grade school on up. By all accounts, the future could not be in more capable hands.

by leg injuries, and they could not keep up with Thomas, Johnson, and Dumars, who earned MVP honors by averaging 27 points a game in the four-game sweep. The following season, the Pistons survived a playoff battle against Jordan and the fast-improving Bulls to reach the finals for a third consecutive season. There they met and defeated the Portland Trailblazers with ease.

With the Lakers aging, the rising team in the West seemed to be the Blazers. Buck Williams, who had labored valiantly for years for mediocre New Jersey Nets teams, had come to Portland to give the team rebounding, interior defense, and leadership. Playmaker Terry Porter emerged as a valuable point guard, and Cliff Robinson, Jerome Kersey, and Kevin Duckworth matured into a serviceable front line. The player who made the Blazers go, however, was Clyde Drexler. The 6'7" Drexler could play any one of four positions, though he was most comfortable as the off-guard, where he could drive the lane or pepper defenses with jump shots. His college nickname, "Clyde the Glide," was quite fitting in the NBA, as he threw down dunk after dunk as the finisher on the Portland fast break. Drexler would take the Blazers back to the NBA finals in 1992, then reunite with former college teammate Hakeem Olajuwon to bring the Houston Rockets an NBA championship in 1995.

The Blazers, however, would always find a superior team standing between them and an NBA title. After Detroit's back-to-back championships, the Chicago Bulls were ready to take center stage. Coach Phil Jackson, who learned his craft as a super sub for Red Holzman's Knickerbocker teams, convinced his players that they needed to do something more than stand around and admire Michael Jordan. For too many years the Bulls had been dumped in the playoffs by opponents who ganged up on Jordan and dared his teammates to win the game. Jackson devised a series of offensive sets, including a special "triangle" offense, that would require everyone on the court to get involved. This in turn forced other teams to spread themselves thin, which gave Jordan and his teammates more room to operate. Almost immediately, forward Scottie Pippen emerged as a bona fide superstar. He shot with supreme confidence, handled the ball with great skill, and rebounded as well as any small forward in the league. And he played suffocating defense. In time, Pippen would be recognized as one of the finest all-around players in basketball history. Joining Pippen on Chicago's front line was Horace Grant, a rugged rebounder whose greatest asset was the intelligence to play within his own limitations. Grant could not pass or dribble, so he never did; he could not shoot outside of 10 feet, so he never did. What he did do was grab 10 rebounds a game and shoot nearly 60 percent from in close, where the Bulls desperately needed a little consistency. At center, veteran Bill Cartwright provided adequate defense and rebounding, though the importance of this position was greatly diminished because of Chicago's other personnel. With Jordan and Pippen penetrating at will, the long-range shooting was left to guards John Paxson and Craig Hodges. When the two Bulls stars kicked the ball back out to these players, they had wide-open shots from the three-point line, and this became a major component of the Chicago attack.

The Bulls put it all together during the 1990–91 season, winning 61 games and outscoring their opponents by nearly 750 points. They wiped out the Knicks, 76ers, and Pistons in the playoffs, then met the Lakers in the finals. A year earlier, Jordan and Magic Johnson agreed to stage a one-on-one battle for pay-per-view television, but the league shut them down. This time, America would get to see them go head-to-head in the NBA finals. Unfortunately, the anticipated duel between Michael and Magic never materialized. Los Angeles won the first game on a Sam Perkins buzzer-beater, but then the roof fell in and the Bulls swept the next four. The victory was especially sweet for Jordan.

He was considered in most circles to be the best basketball player ever to lace up a pair of sneakers, but many of his admirers also whispered that he was not a "winner." Jordan had showed them otherwise, although he was far from finished.

Chicago won it all again in 1991–92, defeating the Portland Trailblazers in the finals. No matter what the Blazers tried, the Bulls had an answer. Jordan scored 35 in the first half of Game 1 and canned six three-pointers to set the tone for the rest of the series. In Game 6, the Bulls erased a 17-point deficit when coach Jackson pulled his regulars and instructed his bench-warmers to play catch-up. With Jordan cheering from the bench, the Bulls closed the gap, then he came back in to finish Portland off. With a second straight NBA crown, Chicago began thinking "three-peat."

The Bulls advanced to the 1993 NBA finals, where the Phoenix Suns stood between them and a third consecutive championship. The Suns were led by guard Kevin Johnson and forward Charles Barkley, who had come to the Suns in a trade and unseated Jordan as league MVP. Phoenix played the Bulls extremely tough, losing two close games to open the series then coming back with a wild triple-overtime victory in Game 3. Jordan took over in Game 4 and scored 55 points, including a clutch three-pointer to seal the Chicago victory. Barkley whipped his team into shape for Game 5 and the Suns destroyed the Bulls, and in Game 6 Phoenix had the ball and was up by two with under a minute to play. An air ball by Dan Majerle gave Chicago possession, and with four seconds left Grant kicked the ball out to Paxson, who buried a three-pointer for a stunning win. A Celtic-like dynasty truly appeared to be in the making. For the first time in 27 years, the NBA had a three-time champion. Jordan had become the undisputed king of the finals, breaking Jerry West's old record by averaging 41 points per game against Phoenix. And there was absolutely nothing to suggest that the Bulls would not keep winning.

Then, in the fall of 1993, Michael Jordan stunned the sports world by announcing that he would retire to play professional baseball. The summer after the Chicago three-peat had not been a good one for Jordan. His father, James, was murdered in his car when he pulled off the highway to take a nap. Then reports began to emerge that Jordan was losing enormous amounts of money playing high-stakes golf. When the media tried to connect the two—suggesting that somehow Jordan had been responsible for his father's death—that was the last straw. He decided he needed a break. Why baseball? James Jordan had always wanted his son to try it.

In Jordan's absence, the Bulls sputtered, opening up all sorts of possibilities and shifting the spotlight to the league's up-and-coming young stars. The NBA had become a savvy marketing machine by this point, and the league jumped on the opportunity to shove players such as Shaquille O'Neal, Alonzo Mourning, Larry Johnson, Reggie Miller, Derrick Coleman, and David Robinson in front of the media as potential champions.

As it turned out, the 1994 NBA championship would come down to a clash between a couple of "old-timers," Patrick Ewing and Hakeem Olajuwon. Ewing had indeed turned the Knicks around after becoming the NBA's first lottery pick in 1985, but the Pistons and Bulls had always

Hakeem Olajuwon's jump hook is just an inch or two better than the defense of New York's Charles Smith and Patrick Ewing in Game 1 of the 1994 NBA Finals. The series would go much the same way, with the Rockets edging the Knicks in seven games.

blocked New York's path to the finals. When Pat Riley quit the Lakers and signed to coach the Knicks in 1991–92, he surrounded Ewing with a mix of talented and aggressive complimentary players, including sharp-shooting John Starks and hard-nosed forwards Charles Oakley and Anthony Mason. Houston Rockets coach Rudy Tomjanovich did the same for Olajuwon, utilizing forwards Otis Thorpe and Robert Horry and a quartet of guards, including Kenny Smith, Vernon Maxwell, Mario Elie, and rookie Sam Cassell. The two clubs met in the finals, and went at each other with basically the same offensive philosophy—a combination of inside scoring and long-distance shooting, with tough interior defense. The Knicks had a chance to win the series in Game 6 with a last-second three-point attempt by Starks, but Olajuwon left Ewing and raced to the perimeter to block the shot and force a seventh game. Starks went cold in the decisive battle, while Maxwell and Cassell had huge games. This proved the difference in a 90-84 Houston victory.

Incredibly, the Houston Rockets repeated as NBA champions in 1995, despite making one of the riskiest and most heavily criticized trades in league history. The defending NBA champs were playing sluggish .500 basketball during the first half of the 1994–95 season, so in February the decision was made to shake things up. Houston traded Thorpe, a valuable rebounder and shot-blocker, along with a first-round draft pick, to the Portland Trailblazers for veteran Clyde Drexler. The idea was to create a running game, which meant that young Horry would see more minutes and Maxwell would see more bench time, now that Drexler was the team's new shooting guard.

Houston's opponents all but wrote them off after the trade—Thorpe was viewed by other NBA players as the man who enabled Olajuwon to operate so effectively away from the basket. Drexler, whose play had declined along with Portland's fortunes, was considered over the hill. But Clyde the Glide snapped back to life and by season's end the Rockets were firing on all cylinders. Houston proved especially resilient in the playoffs, when both the Utah Jazz and Phoenix Suns pushed them to the brink of elimination. Against the Spurs in the conference finals, Drexler baffled the San Antonio defense, and Olajuwon completely outplayed David Robinson, the league's MVP. The Rockets met the Orlando Magic for the NBA championship and Olajuwon gave young Shaquille O'Neal a lesson in clutch play and team leadership during a surprising four-game sweep.

Orlando's presence in the final was something of a surprise to NBA fans. Michael Jordan had returned from his baseball-playing adventure in time to play the last 17 games with the Bulls. Although it took him a while to get his timing back, Jordan seemed ready to take Chicago all the way. But perhaps the Bulls were not ready. Having played the better part of two seasons without him, the team failed to mesh and fell to the Magic in the conference semifinals.

For the 1995–96 season, coach Jackson had a new cast of characters to complement Jordan and Pippen, and Chicago rolled to the best record in NBA history. Bill Cartwright had retired, leaving the Bulls without a veteran to lay down the law in the middle, so Jackson decided to go with a trio of players who could be shuffled in and out of the lineup as situations dictated. Luc Longley, Will Perdue, and Bill Wennington were

An inside force very much in the Wilt Chamberlain mode, Shaquille O'Neal has, like Chamberlain, had trouble translating his immense talent into an NBA championship.

all journeymen centers who lacked the physical skills to be anything more than backups. But the knowledge they had acquired during their careers—along with Jackson's coaching—helped them become an effective three-headed center. At guard, Paxson and B. J. Armstrong were gone, replaced by long-distance shooter Steve Kerr and Ron Harper, who had been written off by most teams after blowing out his knee and toiling for several years with the lowly L.A. Clippers. Also in the mix was 6'11" Toni Kukoc, a Croatian-born international star who could hit from anywhere on the court and play both guard and forward. The final ingredient to this team was Dennis Rodman, who had become the NBA's most flamboyant, outspoken, and eccentric star since leaving the Pistons in 1993. Despite his odd behavior and disruptive influence, he could rebound like no forward in NBA history and at heart loved winning, team-oriented basketball. Jackson believed he could blend Rodman's personality and talent into the Bulls without tearing them apart.

The season began in the new United Center, with the Bulls playing host to the Charlotte Hornets. Jordan erased any doubts about his skills by scoring 42 points, seemingly without effort. The rest of the team took Jordan's cue and they attacked the season as if they too had something to prove. It became clear fairly early that, barring injuries, the Bulls would kill whoever they met in the playoffs. So the big drama for most of 1995–96 was to see whether the team could break the record of 69 wins set by the Lakers back in 1972. Almost unnoticed was the fact that Pippen, who had the team "taken away from him" when Jordan returned, sucked it up and played some of the best basketball anyone had ever seen. Although Jordan was a shoo-in for the 1996 MVP, it could have gone to Pippen. He seemed to soak up each game and get a feel for what the team needed. Then, whatever it was—scoring, defense, rebounding, ball movement, shot-blocking—he went out and did it.

The quest for 70 wins was nearly sidetracked by Rodman, who head-butted an official while arguing a call and was suspended for six games. The Bulls persevered and won number 70 the day Rodman returned to the lineup. They reeled off two more victories to finish with a record of 72–10. As expected, the postseason was little more than a coronation ceremony, as the Miami Heat, New York Knicks, and Orlando Magic won a total of one game against Chicago in the conference playoffs. In the finals, the Bulls defeated a feisty-but-overmatched Seattle squad 4–2. Jordan, who had dedicated his comeback to his murdered father, wept openly. He had won his fourth championship on Father's Day.

The next season saw the Bulls trample the competition yet again, despite the fact that several Eastern Conference teams stocked themselves with talent in hopes of ambushing Chicago in the playoffs. The Knicks signed shooting guard Allan Houston, making Starks into the league's top sixth man, and added Larry Johnson and Buck Williams to a frontcourt that already featured Ewing and Oakley. The Hawks acquired Dikembe Mutombo and Christian Laettner to go with their crack guard combination of Steve Smith and Mookie Blaylock. And the Heat put together a nice team under coach Pat Riley, who left the Knicks after they failed to return to the finals in 1995. Alonzo Mourning, Tim Hardaway, Ja-

The Chicago Bulls of the 1990s—rarely tested in the playoffs, and winners of an amazing 72 games in 1995–96—have dominated the NBA like no team since the Boston Celtics of the 1960s. Cradling five of the team's championship trophies are, left to right, Dennis Rodman, Michael Jordan, Scottie Pippen, Ron Harper, and coach Phil Jackson.

mal Mashburn, Voshon Lenard, and Dan Majerle made up as good a starting five as any team could offer, but they were lucky to get one game from the Bulls in the conference finals. In the Western Conference, Karl Malone and John Stockton, who had labored together for a decade trying to get the Utah Jazz to the top, had raised their games another notch, with Malone wresting the league MVP from Jordan and the Jazz advancing to the championship series. Try as they might, however, the Jazz had no answer for Jordan and Pippen, who combined to average over 50 points a game in Chicago's 4–2 victory.

Despite five championships in seven seasons, the Chicago Bulls did not dominate the thoughts of pro basketball fans the way the Celtics had in the midst of their great run. The NBA had become far too smart to let that happen. The league had an unprecedented number of high-profile stars to market during the 1990s, and this it did exceedingly well.

A quartet of first-rate centers entered the league beginning in 1989, when David Robinson fulfilled his obligation to the Navy and joined the San Antonio Spurs. A remarkably fluid and graceful player for his size, he led the NBA in scoring, free throws, rebounding, and blocked shots at various times during the 1990s. Robinson has also been honored as Rookie of the Year, Defensive Player of the Year, and league MVP. Dikembe Mutombo was an immediate defensive force when he joined the Denver Nuggets in 1991, and steadily improved his shot-blocking and rebounding skills. Somewhat limited in his offense repertoire, Mutombo worked hard until he could hit more than half of his shots from the field. He won the NBA Defensive Player of the Year award in 1995, and again in 1997 after signing as a free agent with Hawks. His presence in the post allowed Christian Laettner to play power forward, which ignited a resurgence by the long-dormant Hawks in 1997–98.

In the fall of 1992, O'Neal and Mourning came into the league, sparking anticipation of a Chamberlain-Russell rivalry. O'Neal may be the most awesome physical specimen ever to play in the NBA. Standing 7'1" and weighing 325 pounds, he overwhelmed the league's top centers in his rookie year and took the Orlando Magic to the NBA Finals in just his third season. In 1994–95 he led the league in scoring with a 29.3 average. As with all players of his stature, O'Neal was a target for criticism, most of which revolved around his off-court activities. Shaq's success as a rap singer and movie star had a lot of basketball people wondering whether he did

Point guard John Stockton and power forward Karl Malone, two of the best at their positions in the NBA's history. The Utah Jazz's dynamic duo have been trying to climb the championship mountain for more than a decade.

everything he could to maximize his potential. The comparisons to Chamberlain—good and bad—continued when Shaq signed with the Lakers in 1996. Mourning, a defensive specialist, showed a real talent for shot-blocking and rebounding as a rookie, and his intensity and ability to run the floor drew comparisons to Russell. A 1995 trade saw Mourning go from the Charlotte Hornets to the Heat, where coach Pat Riley worked with him to improve his offensive skills.

Among the forwards knocking on the door of greatness during the 1990s were Karl Malone and Grant Hill. Malone packed a small forward's skills into a power forward's body, with his ability to finish the break and hit clutch shots from 12 to 15 feet. The main man on the Utah Jazz, he topped the 2,000-point mark every year from 1987–88 to 1996–97, a pro record. A perennial All-NBA forward, Malone finally won the MVP in 1997, when he led the Jazz to the NBA finals. Malone's combination of strength, quickness, and running ability made him one of the hardest players in history to keep from scoring, as well as the finest power forward ever to play the game. Hill, who took his phenomenal college game and bumped it up a notch in the pros, earned a spot next to Pippen as the game's top small forward. The floor general of the Detroit Pistons even as a rookie, Hill was allowed to ignite the team's offense with his great one-on-one moves. A smart defensive player, he improved steadily from the day he came into the NBA and within three seasons ranked among the top two or three defenders at the small forward position.

As for the guard position, it went two ways during the 1990s: big and small. Following on the heels of big guards like Magic Johson, Jordan, and Drexler was Anfernee Hardaway. Hardaway came into the league with the Orlando Magic in 1993 as a 6'7" point guard, and drew immediate comparisons to Magic Johnson. He could score from long distance, hit clutch shots from a dozen different angles, and back his man down toward the foul line before making his move. He and Johnson probably rate as the only two point guards in history who could post up against power forwards and live to tell about it.

Playing much smaller during the 1990s—but contributing just as big—were John Stockton and Gary Payton. Stockton and Malone hooked up to become the most effective guard-forward combo since Oscar Robertson and Jerry Lucas, leading the Jazz to the playoffs every year they played together. Though never a flashy guard, Stockton knew what it took to run a team—when to force the action, when to let up, when to give a guy a shot, and when to take one for the team. A smart and opportunistic cutter, Stockton over the years probably got nearly as many passes for layups from Malone as he delivered to the "Mailman." Payton, the top defensive guard in the NBA during the 1990s, was a major reason why the Seattle Supersonics reached the 1996 NBA finals, and a major reason why they fell short in other years. Though his combined offensive and defensive skills ranked among the best ever at his position, his decision-making at the point was sometimes inconsistent. The Sonics, however, knew they had one of the most valuable commodities in the league, and chose to build around Payton instead of their other stars. Such is life in the new NBA. Guards can bully forwards, forwards can outshoot guards, centers throw in 20-

footers, and point men need an occasional passing lesson.

As the NBA nears the turn of the century, a new constellation of stars is appearing on the horizon. The basketball talent in the United States has become so advanced that many players have NBA-level skills in high school. Many, of course, are going right into the NBA—while others accept college scholarships so they can beef up or get a year or two of seasoning. The question is, how advanced is their understanding of the game? On a pure skills level, Allen Iverson, Kobe Bryant, Stephon Marbury, Kevin Garnett, Shareef Abdur-Rahim and other young guns seem perfectly at home in the NBA. Only time will tell whether they possess the ability to grow their games, make adjustments, and rise as whole players to meet the challenges and demands of championship-level basketball.

They do have one important thing going for them: A few years ahead of them are the players who are expected to take the torch of leadership that has been handed down from Mikan to Cousy to Russell to West to Kareem to Bird and Magic and finally to Jordan. How players like Grant Hill, Juwan Howard, Tim Duncan, and Antonio McDyess do under the microscope should give the next generation of superstars a road map of success and failure. Which route they choose will determine who takes the game into its third century.

Passing the torch: Michael Jordan advises his heir apparent, Kobe Bryant of the Lakers, during a lull in the action.

A Basketball Timeline

1891 Dr. James Naismith introduces his new game to a group of secretarial students at the Springfield YMCA.

1892 The term "basket-ball" is first used.

1893 College—The first women's college game is played by two intramural teams at Smith College.

1894 The first basketball is manufactured by a company in Chicopee Falls, Massachusetts; the free throw line is moved from 20 to 15 feet; the University of Chicago completes the first basketball "season" with a 6–1 record against local clubs.

1895 College—The value of a basket is changed from three points to two; the Minnesota State School of Agriculture defeats Hamline College in the first intercollegiate basketball game, 9–3.

1896 College—The first five-on-five game is played between Chicago and Iowa; the first backboards are put in use.

Pro—The Brooklyn and Trenton clubs compete in the first professional basketball game.

1897 The Amateur Athletic Union holds its first basketball tournament, which is won by a team from the 23rd Street YMCA in New York City.

1898 Pro—The first National Basketball League is formed, with teams in New Jersey and Pennsylvania.

1901 Pro—The New York Wanderers join the NBL and win the league championship. The Buffalo Germans win the AAU championship at the Pan American Exposition.

1902 Pro—The Philadelphia Basketball League is formed.

1903 Pro—The New England Basketball League and Western Massachusetts Basketball League are formed.

1904 College—Sam Ransom of Beloit College in Wisconsin becomes the first black man to play on a varsity basketball team.

Pro—The Buffalo Germans turn professional and begin barnstorming.

1905 College—Christian Steinmetz of Chicago becomes the first player to score 1,000 points in a career.

1908 A player dribbling the basketball is allowed to stop and shoot; double-dribbling is outlawed in college.

1909 College—Cum Posey, who will become one of the major figures in black sports, makes the Penn State varsity.

Pro—The Eastern League, which operates as a professional circuit until 1933, begins play; the Hudson River League, with top teams in Troy and Kingston, is formed.

1913 Balls no longer have to be poked out of the basket, as the modern drop-through net is introduced.

1915 **College**—Paul Robeson makes the Rutgers basketball team, becoming just the eighth recorded black player to make a college varsity.

Pro—The Edmonton Commercial Grads become basketball's first women's barnstorming team.

1916 **Pro**—The New York Celtics begin playing for money.

1917 Converse debuts its All-Star basketball shoe.

1921 **College**—The first conference tournament—held by the Southern Conference—is won by Kentucky.

Pro—A game between the Celtics and Whirlwinds in New York City draws 11,000 fans.

1923 **College**—The designated free-throw shooter is eliminated; instead, the player fouled must take his own shots.

Pro—Bob Douglas forms the Harlem Renaissance basketball team.

1924 **High School**—Marie Boyd of Maryland's Lonaconing Central High scores 156 points in a women's contest.

1925 **High School**—Passaic High wins its 159th game in a row.

Pro—The American Basketball League is formed; the double-dribble is banned by the ABL, eliminating the one major difference between the college and pro games.

1927 **Pro**—The Original Celtics join the ABL and win the league championship. Abe Saperstein forms the Harlem Globetrotters.

1928 **High School**—Kentucky's Carr Creek High School, with an enrollment of eight male students, reaches the state finals but loses in quadruple-overtime.

College—Referees begin calling "charging" fouls on dribblers.

1929 **High School**—The first All-America team is selected.

1930 The size of an official ball is reduced by one inch and one ounce to 31 inches around and 22 ounces.

1931 **College**—A charity triple-header in Madison Square Garden draws 15,000 fans.

Pro—The American Basketball League folds. The Dallas Golden Cyclones, led by 16-year-old Babe Didrikson, win the AAU Women's championship.

1932 **College**—John Wooden of Purdue is history's first three-time All-American.

1933 **College**—A seven-game marathon draws 20,000 fans to

Madison Square Garden, with proceeds going to charity.

1934 The size of the ball is reduced again, to approximately 30 inches around.

College—Ned Irish begins promoting college double-headers at Madison Square Garden. Freshman Hank Luisetti unveils his running one-handed shot at Stanford University.

1935 **High School**—The first national tournament for black high-school teams is held at the Tuskegee Institute.

College—The modern three-second rule goes into effect; jump balls after made free throws are eliminated—the team scored upon takes the ball out beneath its basket.

Pro—The Midwest Basketball Conference—forerunner of the successful NBL—begins play.

1936 **Olympics**—James Naismith watches as the USA takes the gold medal and his home country of Canada wins the silver in the first Olympic basketball competition, held in Berlin, Germany.

1937 **College**—The jump ball after each basket is eliminated prior to the 1937–38 season.

Pro—The National Basketball League is formed.

1938 **College**—Temple University wins the first National Invitation Tournament.

1939 **College**—The University of Oregon wins the first NCAA Tournament.

1940 **College**—The first live television broadcast of a basketball game features Fordham vs. Pittsburgh.

1943 **College**—Wyoming (31–2) becomes the first college team to win 30 games in a season.

1944 **College**—Defensive goaltending is no longer allowed; players get five fouls before being disqualified; unlimited substitutions are made legal.

1945 **Pro**—Mel Riebe of the Cleveland Allmen Transfers and Bobby McDermott of the Ft. Wayne Zollner Pistons become the first two players to average more than 20 points in a season.

1946 **College**—Seven-footer Bob Kurland helps Oklahoma State become the first back-to-back winner of the NCAA Tournament; fans get a better view of the action thanks to transparent backboards.

Pro—The Basketball Association of America in founded. Holcombe Rucker starts a summer league in New York City, which becomes the premier "open" tournament in the country.

1947 **College**—Don Barksdale of UCLA is the first black consensus All-American.

1948 **College**—Coaches are allowed to talk to their players during time-outs for the first time.

Pro—The all-black New York Rens join the NBL as the Dayton Rens, taking over for the defunct Detroit Vagabond Kings.

1949 **College**—The Associated Press publishes its first college basketball poll.

Pro—Joe Fulks scores 63 points against Indianapolis, setting a mark that will hold up for more than a decade; George Mikan becomes the first pro to average better than 25 points a game; the National Basketball League and Basketball Association of American merge into the National Basketball Association.

1950 **College**—CCNY wins the NCAA and NIT tournaments.

Pro—Chuck Cooper (Boston Celtics) and Earl Lloyd (Washington Capitols) become the first black college players drafted by the pros, and Sweetwater Clifton of the Harlem Globetrotters is signed by the New York Knicks; Red Auerbach is hired to coach the Boston Celtics.

1951 **College**—A point-shaving scandal casts a shadow over college basketball and drives many fans to watch pro basketball for the first time.

Pro—East beats West in the first NBA All-Star Game, as Boston center Ed Macauley takes home MVP honors; George Mikan of the Lakers wins the NBA scoring title for third consecutive year.

1952 **Pro**—Bobby Wanzer of the Royals becomes the first player to hit more than 90% of his free throws.

1953 **Pro**—Bob Cousy of the Celtics sinks a record 30 free throws and becomes the first NBA player to score 50 points in a post-season game during a wild, quadruple-overtime contest against the Syracuse Nationals.

1954 **High School**—Milan High—subject of the 1986 film *Hoosiers*—reaches the Indiana state finals; Chicago's all-black Du Sable High reaches the Illinois state finals.

College—Bevo Francis scores a record 113 points in a game for Rio Grande College; Frank Selvy also scores 100, and becomes the first player to average more than 40 points a game; Kentucky, placed on probation the season before, declines an invitation to the NCAA tournament, despite a 25–0 record; the NCAA championship game is televised nationally for the first time; the modern one-and-one free-throw rule is introduced.

Pro—The NBA institutes the 24-second clock; the Baltimore Bullets, league champs in 1948, go bankrupt and leave the NBA 14 games into the season; the Minneapolis Lakers win their fifth pro championship in six seasons.

1955 **College**—Phil Woolpert of the University of San Francisco is the first UPI Coach of the Year.

Pro—The Hawks move from Milwaukee to St. Louis. Nera White, the greatest star in women's basketball, is named an AAU All-American for the first of 15 consecutive times.

1956 **College**—George Washington University becomes the first team to make half its shots during a season; Bill Russell and K.C. Jones lead the University of San Francisco to 55 straight victories and a second consecutive NCAA title; the free throw lane is widened from 6 to 12 feet.

Pro—Bob Pettit of the Hawks wins the inaugural MVP Award.

1957 **College**—North Carolina goes 32–0, including a triple-overtime win against Wilt Chamberlain and Kansas in the NCAA final; offensive goaltending is no longer allowed.

Pro—The Pistons move from Ft. Wayne to Detroit and the Royals move from Rochester to Cincinnati.

1958 **Pro**—George Yardley of the Pistons become the first pro to score more than 2,000 points in a season.

1959 **Pro**—Bob Cousy dishes out a record 19 assists in one half.

1960 **High School**—Danny Heater of Burnsville High in West Virginia scores 135 points in a game.

College—Oscar Robertson of the University of Cincinnati wins his third straight Player of the Year Award.

Pro—Wilt Chamberlain is named NBA Rookie of the Year and MVP; Bob Cousy leads the league in assists for the eighth consecutive year; Bill Russell hauls down 40 rebounds in a game against the Hawks in the NBA finals; the NBA goes west as the Lakers move from Minneapolis to Los Angeles.

1961 **Pro**—Wilt Chamberlain becomes the first pro to score more than 3,000 points in a season; Bill Sharman of the Celtics leads the league in free-throw percentage for the seventh time; the Chicago Packers join the NBA.

1962 **International**—Suleiman Ali Nashnush of the Libyan national team becomes basketball's first eight-foot-tall player.

College—Arkansas guard Tommy Boyer, who is blind in one eye, sets an NCAA record with 93.3% foul shooting; Jerry Lucas of Ohio State leads the nation in field-goal percentage for the third year in a row.

Pro—Wilt Chamberlain of the Philadelphia Warriors scores 100 points against the Knicks and averages 50.4 points per game over the season; Elgin Baylor burns the Celtics for 61 points during the NBA finals; the Warriors move to San Francisco following the 1961–62 season; the Packers change their name to the Zephyrs; the American Basketball League begins its one and only season of operation.

1963 **Pro**—Bill Russell of the Celtics becomes the first player to win the NBA MVP three times in a row; the Chicago Zephyrs become the Baltimore Bullets and the Syracuse Nationals become the Philadelphia 76ers prior to the 1963–64 season.

1964 **Pro**—24-year-old Dave DeBusschere becomes player-coach of the Pistons.

1966 **College**—Texas Western starts five black players in the NCAA final and defeats all-white Kentucky.

Pro—The Chicago Bulls join the NBA; Wilt Chamberlain of the 76ers wins the NBA scoring title for the sixth straight season; the Celtics win their eighth consecutive NBA title.

1967 **College**—Dunking is declared illegal.

Pro—Wilt Chamberlain goes 18-18 from the field against the Bullets; the American Basketball Association begins play; the San Diego Rockets and Seattle Supersonics join the NBA; the New Jersey Americans move to Long Island and become the New York Nets.

1968 **College**—More than 52,000 fans watch as Elvin Hayes of the University of Houston scores 39 points to end UCLA's 47-game winning streak.

Pro—East beats West in the first ABA All-Star Game, as guard Larry Brown takes home MVP honors; Earl Monroe of the Bullets sets a record for rookie guards with 56 points against the Lakers; Bill Russell, the NBA's first black head coach, leads the Celtics to the league title; the Hawks move from St. Louis to Atlanta and the Phoenix Suns join the NBA prior to the 1968–69 season.

1969 **College**—Lew Alcindor is named Most Outstanding Player in the NCAA Tournament for the third year in a row.

Pro—Wilt Chamberlain tops the 60-point mark twice in two weeks, marking the 32nd time his career he reached that plateau; Wes Unseld of the Bullets is named NBA MVP and Rookie of the Year; Jerry West of the Lakers wins the first NBA Finals MVP Award, despite playing for the losing team; University of Detroit junior Spencer Haywood declares himself a hardship case and leaves college to sign with the ABA Denver Rockets prior to the 1969–70 season.

1970 **College**—Pete Maravich of LSU averages more than 40 points a game for the third year in a row; Austin Carr of Notre Dame sets an NCAA tournament record with 61 points against Ohio.

Pro—Rookie Spencer Haywood leads the ABA in scoring and rebounding, and wins the MVP award; the Cleveland Cavaliers, Buffalo Braves, and Portland Trailblazers join the NBA.

1971 Women's rules reduce team sides from six players to five.

Pro—The San Francisco Warriors move to Oakland and take the name Golden State and the Rockets move from San Diego to Houston.

1972 **International**—The USSR wins the gold medal on a disputed last-second shot, ending the USA's hold on the gold medal.

College—Immaculata defeats West Chester State in the first AIAW intercollegiate women's championship game; freshmen are declared eligible for varsity play for the 1972–73 season.

Pro—The Los Angeles Lakers win 33 games in a row on their way to the NBA championship; the Indiana Pacers become the ABA's first repeat champions; the Cincinnati Royals become the Kansas City–Omaha Kings.

1973 **College**—UCLA wins its seventh straight NCAA Title.

Pro—Wilt Chamberlain of the Lakers wins his 11th and final rebounding title and also becomes the first player to make more than 70% of his shots from the field in a season; the ABA Dallas Chaparrals become the San Antonio Spurs and the NBA Baltimore Bullets become the Capital Bullets; center Elmore Smith of the Lakers swats a record 17 shots in a game.

1974 **College**—UCLA wins its 88th game in a row; Tennessee and Temple combine for just 17 points as both teams run stalling offenses all game long.

Pro—The New Orleans Jazz join the NBA and the Capital Bullets become the Washington Bullets; the ABA Denver Rockets change their name to the Nuggets.

1975 **College**—The term Final Four begins to appear in NCAA literature.

Pro—George McGinnis of the Pacers and Julius Erving of the Nets are named ABA co-MVPs; the Kings abandon Omaha.

1976 **International**—The USSR captures the gold medal in the first Olympic women's basketball competition.

College—Indiana goes 32–0 and wins the national championship; dunking is legalized for the 1976–77 season.

Pro—The NBA and ABA agree to merge for the 1976–77 season; the Nets sell Julius Erving to the Philadelphia 76ers so they can afford to join the NBA; an out-of-court settlement between the NBA and Players Association leads to free agency; Spurs forward Larry Kenon establishes an NBA record with 11 steals in a game.

1977 **Pro**—The New York Nets move to New Jersey.

1978 **Pro**—David Thompson of the Nuggets sets a record for guards with 73 points against the Pistons on the final day of the 1977–78 season; the Buffalo Braves move to San Diego and are renamed the Clippers.

1979 **College**—Demand for NCAA tournament tickets becomes so great that a public lottery is held for the first time; Magic Johnson and Larry Bird meet in the NCAA final, drawing the largest television viewing audience in basketball history.

Pro—Kevin Porter of the Pistons reaches the 25-assist mark for the third time in his career; Moses Malone of the Rockets becomes the first ex-ABA player to win the NBA MVP; the NBA adopts the three-point shot for the 1979–80 season.

1980 **International**—Yugoslavia becomes the first country other than the USA and USSR to win an Olympic gold medal in basketball.

College—Center Steve Johnson of Oregon State becomes the first college player to shoot better than 70% from the field.

Pro—The Dallas Mavericks join the NBA.

1981 **College**—The NCAA takes control of the women's game from the AIAW.

Pro—Calvin Murphy of the Rockets shoots a record 95.8% from the free-throw line.

1982 **High School**—Cheryl Miller scores 105 points in a game.

College—The first NCAA women's championship is won by Louisiana Tech.

1983 **Pro**—Randy Smith of the Clippers plays in his 906th straight game; Moses Malone leads the NBA in offensive rebounds a record seventh time; David Stern becomes NBA Commissioner.

1984 **International**—The U.S. wins its first gold medal in women's basketball.

College—Cheryl Miller leads USC to a second-straight NCAA title.

Pro—Larry Nance of the Cavaliers wins the NBA's first All-Star Slam Dunk Contest; Darryl Dawkins of the Nets commits a record 386 fouls in one season; the Clippers move from San Diego to Los Angeles; the NBA and Players Association reach an agreement that guarantees the players a 53% cut of the league's gross revenues in return for a salary cap.

1985 **College**—Forward Xavier McDaniel of Wichita State becomes the first player to lead the nation in both scoring and rebounding during the same season; the NCAA tournament field is expanded to 64 teams; the NCAA adopts the 45-second clock.

Pro—The Lakers shoot 54.5% from the field in 1984–85 to establish an all-time record; the Kings move from Kansas City to Sacramento. Lynette Woodard becomes the first woman to play for the Harlem Globetrotters.

1986 COLLEGE—The NCAA adopts the three-point shot.

PRO—Larry Bird wins the first All-Star Weekend Long Distance Shootout; Alvin Robertson of the Bucks sets a new record with 301 steals; Michael Jordan sets a post-season record with 63 points against the Celtics; Nancy Lieberman plays for the USBL Springfield Fame to become the first woman to appear in an official men's professional game; Detroit scores a record 186 points against the Nuggets in a triple-overtime game.

1987 INTERNATIONAL—Oscar Schmidt of Brazil leads his country to a shocking upset over the U.S. in the Pan Am Games.

1988 PRO—An NBA-record crowd of 61,983 watch the Celtics play the Pistons at the Pontiac Silverdome; Jack Sikma of the Bucks becomes the first center to lead the league in free-throw percentage; the Charlotte Hornets and Miami Heat join the NBA.

1989 INTERNATIONAL—Basketball's international governing body decides to allow pros to compete in the Olympics and other tournaments, setting the stage for the NBA "Dream Team" in the 1992 Olympics.

COLLEGE—Glen Rice of Michigan scores a record 184 points during the NCAA tournament.

PRO—John Sundvold of the Heat becomes the first player to hit more than 50% of his three-point attempts in a season; Kareem Abdul-Jabbar retires with 38,387 career points; the Minnesota Timberwolves and Orlando Magic join the NBA.

1990 HIGH SCHOOL—Lisa Leslie of Morningside High scores 101 in one half.

COLLEGE—A record crowd of 68,112 pays to see LSU battle Notre Dame at the Louisiana Superdome.

PRO—Scott Skiles of the Magic dishes out a record 30 assists in a game.

1991 COLLEGE—Loyola Marymount scores a record 186 points in a game; coach Eddie Sutton takes his fourth (Creighton, Arkansas, Kentucky, and Oklahoma State) team to the NCAA tournament.

PRO—Tim Hardaway of the Warriors sets a record for futility when he goes 0-17 from the field in a game against the Timberwolves.

1992 INTERNATIONAL—The Dream Team, starring Michael Jordan, Magic Johnson, Charles Barkley, and Larry Bird, wins the gold medal, defeating its rivals by an average of 43 points.

COLLEGE—Shaquille O'Neal of LSU blocks 11 shots in an NCAA tournament game; Duke University becomes the first repeat winner of the NCAA Tournament since UCLA in 1973.

Pro—Magic Johnson comes out of retirement to lead the West to a 153-113 rout in the All-Star Game.

1993 **College**—The shot clock is reduced from 45 to 35 seconds.

Pro—Michael Jordan wins the NBA scoring title a record seventh straight time; the Bulls become the first team to capture three consecutive NBA titles since the Celtics in 1966; at 7'7", Gheorghe Muresan of the Bullets becomes the tallest player in NBA history; Micheal Williams of the Timberwolves hits 97 straight free throws.

1994 **College**—Troy State cans 28 three-pointers in a game against George Mason.

Pro—Jeff Hornacek of the Jazz goes 8-8 from three-point range in a game against the Supersonics.

1995 **College**—The University of Connecticut's men's and women's basketball teams achieve number-one national rankings at the same time.

Pro—Forward Robert Horry of the Rockets gets seven steals against the Magic to set an NBA Finals record; the Toronto Raptors and Vancouver Grizzlies join the NBA.

1996 **Pro**—The Vancouver Grizzlies lose a record 23 games in a row; Lenny Wilkens becomes the first NBA coach to reach 1,000 career victories; John Stockton of the Jazz leads the NBA in assists per game for a record ninth consecutive season.

1997 **Pro**—Dennis Rodman becomes the first player to win six straight rebounding titles; Karl Malone scores 2,000 points for a record 10th consecutive season; Michael Jordan is named NBA Finals MVP for the fifth time; the Washington Bullets change their name to the Wizards; A.C. Green of the Mavericks breaks Randy Smith's record when he plays in his 907th consecutive game.

1998 **College**—Tubby Smith, the first African-American coach hired by the University of Kentucky, wins a national championship in his first season on the job.

Pro—For one game the Indiana Pacers achieve the ultimate blend of offense and defense, beating the Portland Trailblazers 124-59 in the first modern NBA game where one team doubled the score of another. The Chicago Bulls add one more NBA championship to their resume.

APPENDIX A
The NCAA Men's Tournament

Season	Champion	Runner-Up	Final Four Most Outstanding Player
1938–39	Oregon (46)	Ohio State (33)	None Selected
1939–40	Indiana (60)	Kansas (42)	Marv Huffman, Indiana
1940–41	Wisconsin (39)	Washington State (34)	John Kotz, Wisconsin
1941–42	Stanford (53)	Dartmouth (38)	Howie Dallmar, Stanford
1942–43	Wyoming (46)	Georgetown (34)	Ken Sailors, Wyoming
1943–44	Utah (42 [OT])	Dartmouth (40)	Arnie Ferrin, Utah
1944–45	Oklahoma State (49)	NYU (45)	Bob Kurland, Oklahoma State
1945–46	Oklahoma State (43)	UNC (40)	Bob Kurland, Oklahoma State
1946–47	Holy Cross (58)	Oklahoma (47)	George Kaftan, Holy Cross
1947–48	Kentucky (58)	Baylor (42)	Alex Groza, Kentucky
1948–49	Kentucky (46)	Oklahoma State (36)	Alex Groza, Kentucky
1949–50	CCNY (71)	Bradley (68)	Irwin Dambrot, CCNY
1950–51	Kentucky (68)	Kansas State (58)	None Selected
1951–52	Kansas (80)	St. John's (63)	Clyde Lovellette, Kansas
1952–53	Indiana (69)	Kansas (68)	B. H. Born, Kansas
1953–54	La Salle (92)	Bradley (76)	Tom Gola, La Salle
1954–55	San Francisco (77)	La Salle (63)	Bill Russell, San Francisco
1955–56	San Francisco (83)	Iowa (71)	Hal Lear, Temple
1956–57	UNC (54 [3 OT])	Kansas (53)	Wilt Chamberlain, Kansas
1957–58	Kentucky (84)	Seattle (72)	Elgin Baylor, Seattle
1958–59	California (71)	West Virginia (70)	Jerry West, West Virginia
1959–60	Ohio State (75)	California (55)	Jerry Lucas, Ohio State
1960–61	Cincinnati (70 [OT])	Ohio State (65)	Jerry Lucas, Ohio State
1961–62	Cincinnati (71)	Ohio State (59)	Paul Hogue, Cincinnati
1962–63	Loyola (60 [OT])	Cincinnati (58)	Art Heyman, Duke
1963–64	UCLA (98)	Duke (83)	Walt Hazzard, UCLA
1964–65	UCLA (91)	Michigan (80)	Gail Goodrich, UCLA
1965–66	Texas Western (72)	Kentucky (65)	Jerry Chambers, Texas Western
1966–67	UCLA (79)	Dayton (64)	Lew Alcindor, UCLA
1967–68	UCLA (78)	UNC (55)	Lew Alcindor, UCLA
1968–69	UCLA (92)	Purdue (72)	Lew Alcindor, UCLA
1969–70	UCLA (80)	Jacksonville (69)	Sidney Wicks, UCLA
1970–71	UCLA (68)	Villanova (62)	Howard Porter, Villanova
1971–72	UCLA (81)	Florida State (76)	Bill Walton, UCLA
1972–73	UCLA (87)	Memphis (66)	Bill Walton, UCLA
1973–74	NC State (76)	Marquette (64)	David Thompson, NC State
1974–75	UCLA (92)	Kentucky (85)	Richard Washington, UCLA
1975–76	Indiana (86)	Michigan (68)	Kent Benson, Indiana
1976–77	Marquette (67)	UNC (59)	Butch Lee, Marquette
1977–78	Kentucky (94)	Duke (88)	Jack Givens, Kentucky

1978–79	Michigan State (75)	Indiana State (64)	Magic Johnson, Michigan State
1979–80	Louisville (59)	UCLA (54)	Darrell Griffith, Louisville
1980–81	Indiana (63)	UNC (50)	Isiah Thomas, Indiana
1981–82	UNC (63)	Georgetown (62)	James Worthy, UNC
1982–83	NC State (54)	Houston (52)	Hakeem Olajuwon, Houston
1983–84	Georgetown (84)	Houston (75)	Patrick Ewing, Georgetown
1984–85	Villanova (66)	Georgetown (64)	Ed Pinckney, Villanova
1985–86	Louisville (72)	Duke (69)	Pervis Ellison, Louisville
1986–87	Indiana (74)	Syracuse (73)	Keith Smart, Indiana
1987–88	Kansas (83)	Oklahoma (79)	Danny Manning, Kansas
1988–89	Michigan (80[OT])	Seton Hall (79)	Glen Rice, Michigan
1989–90	UNLV (103)	Duke (73)	Anderson Hunt, UNLV
1990–91	Duke (72)	Kansas (65)	Christian Laettner, Duke
1991–92	Duke (71)	Michigan (51)	Bobby Hurley, Duke
1992–93	UNC (77)	Michigan (71)	Donald Williams, UNC
1993–94	Arkansas (76)	Duke (72)	Corliss Williamson, Arkansas
1994–95	UCLA (89)	Arkansas (78)	Ed O'Bannon, UCLA
1995–96	Kentucky (76)	Syracuse (67)	Tony Delk, Kentucky
1996–97	Arizona (84 [OT])	Kentucky (79)	Miles Simon, Arizona
1997–98	Kentucky (78)	Utah (69)	Jeff Sheppard, Kentucky

APPENDIX B

Men's College Player of the Year

Season	Player	School
1954–55*	Tom Gola	La Salle
1955–56	Bill Russell	San Francisco
1956–57	Chet Forte	Columbia
1957–58	Oscar Robertson	Cincinnati
1958–59	Oscar Robertson	Cincinnati
1959–60	Oscar Robertson	Cincinnati
1960–61†	Jerry Lucas	Ohio State
1961–62	Jerry Lucas	Ohio State
1962–63	Art Heyman	Duke
1963–64	Gary Bradds	Ohio State
1964–65	Bill Bradley	Princeton
1965–66	Cazzie Russell	Michigan
1966–67	Lew Alcindor	UCLA
1967–68	Elvin Hayes	Houston
1968–69	Lew Alcindor	UCLA
1969–70	Pete Maravich	LSU
1970–71	Austin Carr	Notre Dame
1971–72	Bill Walton	UCLA
1972–73	Bill Walton	UCLA
1973–74	David Thompson	NC State
1974–75	David Thompson	NC State
1975–76	Adrian Dantley	Notre Dame
1976–77‡	Marques Johnson	UCLA
1977–78	Phil Ford	UNC
1978–79	Larry Bird	Indiana State
1979–80	Darrell Griffith	Louisville
1980–81	Danny Ainge	Brigham Young
1981–82	Ralph Sampson	Virginia
1982–83	Ralph Sampson	Virginia
1983–84	Michael Jordan	UNC
1984–85	Chris Mullin	St. John's
1985–86	Walter Berry	St. John's
1986–87	David Robinson	Navy
1987–88	Danny Manning	Kansas
1988–89	Sean Elliott	Arizona
1989–90	Lionel Simmons	La Salle
1990–91	Larry Johnson	UNLV

1991–92	Christian Laettner	Duke
1992–93	Calbert Cheaney	Indiana
1993–94	Glenn Robinson	Purdue
1994–95	Ed O'Bannon	UCLA
1995–96	Marcus Camby	Massachusetts
1996–97	Tim Duncan	Wake Forest
1997–98	Antawn Jamison	UNC

* United Press International
†Associated Press
‡Wooden Award

APPENDIX C

Men's College Statistical Records

(All statistics through 1997–98 season)

Points in a Season

Player	School	Season	Points
Pete Maravich	Louisiana State	1969–70	1,381
Elvin Hayes	Houston	1968–69	1,214
Frank Selvy	Furman	1953–54	1,209
Pete Maravich	Louisiana State	1968–69	1,148
Pete Maravich	Louisiana State	1967–68	1,138
Bo Kimble	Loyola Marymount	1989–90	1,131
Hersey Hawkins	Bradley	1987–88	1,125
Austin Carr	Notre Dame	1969–70	1,106
Austin Carr	Notre Dame	1970–71	1,101
Otis Birdsong	Houston	1976–77	1,090

Rebounds in a Season

Player	School	Season	Rebounds
Walter Dukes	Seton Hall	1952–53	734
Tom Gola	La Salle	1953–54	652
Leroy Wright	Pacific	1958–59	652
Charlie Tyra	Louisville	1955–56	645
Paul Silas	Creighton	1963–64	631
Elvin Hayes	Houston	1967–68	624
Artis Gilmore	Jacksonville	1969–70	621
Tom Gola	La Salle	1954–55	618
Ed Conlin	Fordham	1954–55	612

Assists in a Season

Player	School	Season	Assists
Mark Wade	UNLV	1986–87	406
Avery Johnson	Southern	1987–88	399
Anthony Manuel	Bradley	1987–88	373
Avery Johnson	Southern	1986–87	333
Mark Jackson	St. John's	1985–86	328
Sherman Douglas	Syracuse	1988–89	326
Greg Anthony	UNLV	1990–91	310
Sam Crawford	New Mexico State	1992–93	310
Reid Gettys	Houston	1983–84	309
Carl Golston	Loyola	1984–85	305

APPENDIX D

Women's College Champions

AIAW Champions

Season	Champion
1971–72	Immaculata
1972–73	Immaculata
1973–74	Immaculata
1974–75	Delta State
1975–76	Delta State
1976–77	Delta State
1977–78	UCLA
1978–79	Old Dominion
1979–80	Old Dominion
1980–81	Louisiana Tech
1981–82	Rutgers

NCAA Women's Tournament

Season	Winner	Runner-Up
1981–82	Louisiana Tech (76)	Cheyney (62)
1982–83	Southern California (69)	Louisiana Tech (67)
1983–84	Southern California (72)	Tennessee (61)
1984–85	Old Dominion (70)	Creighton (65)
1985–86	Texas (97)	Southern California (81)

1986–87	Tennessee (67)	Louisiana Tech (44)
1987–88	Louisiana Tech (56)	Auburn (54)
1988–89	Tennessee (76)	Auburn (60)
1989–90	Stanford (88)	Auburn (81)
1990–91	Tennessee (70 [OT])	Virginia (67)
1991–92	Stanford (78)	Western Kentucky (62)
1992–93	Texas Tech (84)	Ohio State (82)
1993–94	North Carolina (60)	Louisiana Tech (59)
1994–95	Connecticut (70)	Tennessee (64)
1995–96	Tennessee (83)	Georgia (65)
1996–97	Tennessee (68)	Old Dominion (59)

APPENDIX E
The Olympics

Women's Medalists

Year	Gold	Silver	Bronze
1976	USSR	USA	Bulgaria
1980	USSR	Bulgaria	Yugoslavia
1984	USA	Rep. of Korea	Canada
1988	USA	Yugoslavia	USSR
1992	Unified Team	China	USA
1996	USA	Brazil	Australia

Men's Medalists

Year	Gold	Silver	Bronze
1936	USA	Canada	Mexico
1948	USA	France	Brazil
1952	USA	USSR	Uruguay
1956	USA	USSR	Uruguay
1960	USA	USSR	Brazil
1964	USA	USSR	Brazil
1968	USA	Yugoslavia	USSR
1972	USSR	USA	Cuba
1976	USA	Yugoslavia	USSR
1980	Yugoslavia	Italy	USSR
1984	USA	Spain	Yugoslavia
1988	USSR	Yugoslavia	USA
1992	USA	Croatia	Lithuania
1996	USA	Yugoslavia	Lithuania

APPENDIX F
Champions of Professional Basketball Leagues

American Basketball League

Season	First Half Winner	Second Half Winner	Champion
1925–26	Brooklyn Arcadians	Cleveland Rosenblums	Cleveland, 3–0
1926–27	Cleveland Rosenblums	Brooklyn Celtics	Brooklyn, 3–0
1927–28	New York Celtics*	Fort Wayne Hoosiers†	New York, 3–1
1928–29	Cleveland Rosenblums	Fort Wayne Hoosiers	Cleveland, 4–0
1929–30	Cleveland Rosenblums	Rochester Centrals	Cleveland, 4–1
1930–31	Brooklyn Visitations	Fort Wayne Hoosiers	Brooklyn, 4–2

*Eastern Division Champ

†Western Division Champ

National Basketball League

Season	Eastern Division	Western Division	Champion
1937–38	Akron Firestone Non-Skids	Oshkosh All-Stars	Akron, 4–1
1938–39	Akron Firestone Non-Skids	Oshkosh All-Stars	Akron, 3–2
1939–40	Akron Firestone Non-Skids	Oshkosh All-Stars	Akron, 3–2
	First Place	**Second Place**	
1940–41	Oshkosh All-Stars	Sheboygan Redskins	Oshkosh, 3–0
1941–42	Oshkosh All-Stars	Ft. Wayne Zollner Pistons	Oshkosh, 2–1
1942–43	Ft. Wayne Zollner Pistons	Sheboygan Redskins	Sheboygan, 2–1
1943–44	Ft. Wayne Zollner Pistons	Sheboygan Redskins	Ft. Wayne, 3–0
	Eastern Division	**Western Division**	
1944–45	Ft. Wayne Zollner Pistons	Sheboygan Redskins	Ft. Wayne, 3–2
1945–46	Ft. Wayne Zollner Pistons	Sheboygan Redskins	Ft. Wayne, 3–0
1946–47	Rochester Royals	Oshkosh All-Stars	Oshkosh, 3–1
1947–48	Rochester Royals	Minneapolis Lakers	Minneapolis, 3–1
1948–49	Anderson Duffey Packers	Oshkosh All-Stars	Anderson, 3–0

World Tournament

Year	Champion	Runner-Up
1939	New York Rens (34)	Oshkosh All-Stars (25)
1940	Harlem Globetrotters (31)	Chicago Bruins (29)
1941	Detroit Eagles (39)	Oshkosh All-Stars (37)
1942	Oshkosh All-Stars (43)	Detroit Eagles (41)
1943	Washington Bears (43)	Oshkosh All-Stars (31)
1944	Ft. Wayne Zollner Pistons (50)	Brooklyn Eagles (33)
1945	Ft. Wayne Zollner Pistons (78)	Dayton Acmes (52)
1946	Ft. Wayne Zollner Pistons (73)	Oshkosh All-Stars (57)
1947	Indianapolis Kautskys (62)	Toledo Jeeps (47)
1948	Minneapolis Lakers (75)	New York Rens (71)

Basketball Association of America

Season	Eastern Division	Western Division	Champion
1946–47	Philadelphia Warriors	Chicago Stags	Washington, 4–1
1947–48	Philadelphia Warriors	Baltimore Bullets	Baltimore, 4–2
1948–49	Washington Capitols	Minneapolis Lakers	Minneapolis, 4–2

National Basketball Association

Season	Eastern Division	Western Division	Champion	Most Valuable Player
1949–50*	Syracuse Nationals	Minneapolis Lakers	Minneapolis, 4–2	
1950–51	New York Knicks	Rochester Royals	Rochester, 4–3	
1951–52	New York Knicks	Minneapolis Lakers	Minneapolis, 4–3	
1952–53	New York Knicks	Minneapolis Lakers	Minneapolis, 4–1	
1953–54	Syracuse Nationals	Minneapolis Lakers	Minneapolis, 4–3	
1954–55	Syracuse Nationals	Ft. Wayne Pistons	Syracuse, 4–3	
1955–56	Philadelphia Warriors	Ft. Wayne Pistons	Philadelphia, 4–1	Bob Pettit
1956–57	Boston Celtics	St. Louis Hawks	Boston, 4–3	Bob Cousy
1957–58	Boston Celtics	St. Louis Hawks	St. Louis, 4–2	Bill Russell
1958–59	Boston Celtics	Minneapolis Lakers	Boston, 4–0	Bob Pettit
1959–60	Boston Celtics	St. Louis Hawks	Boston, 4–3	Wilt Chamberlain
1960–61	Boston Celtics	St. Louis Hawks	Boston, 4–1	Bill Russell
1961–62	Boston Celtics	Los Angeles Lakers	Boston, 4–3	Bill Russell
1962–63	Boston Celtics	Los Angeles Lakers	Boston, 4–2	Bill Russell
1963–64	Boston Celtics	San Francisco Warriors	Boston, 4–1	Oscar Robertson
1964–65	Boston Celtics	Los Angeles Lakers	Boston, 4–1	Bill Russell
1965–66	Boston Celtics	Los Angeles Lakers	Boston, 4–3	Wilt Chamberlain
1966–67	Philadelphia 76ers	San Francisco Warriors	Philadelphia, 4–2	Wilt Chamberlain
1967–68	Boston Celtics	Los Angeles Lakers	Boston, 4–2	Wilt Chamberlain
1968–69	Boston Celtics	Los Angeles Lakers	Boston, 4–3	Wes Unseld
1969–70	New York Knicks	Los Angeles Lakers	New York, 4–3	Willis Reed
	Eastern Conference	**Western Conference**		
1970–71	Baltimore Bullets	Milwaukee Bucks	Milwaukee, 4–0	Kareem Abdul-Jabbar
1971–72	New York Knicks	Los Angeles Lakers	Los Angeles, 4–1	Kareem Abdul-Jabbar
1972–73	New York Knicks	Los Angeles Lakers	New York, 4–1	Dave Cowens
1973–74	Boston Celtics	Milwaukee Bucks	Boston, 4–3	Kareem Abdul-Jabbar
1974–75	Washington Bullets	Golden State Warriors	Golden State, 4–0	Bob McAdoo
1975–76	Boston Celtics	Phoenix Suns	Boston, 4–2	Kareem Abdul-Jabbar
1976–77	Philadelphia 76ers	Portland Trailblazers	Portland, 4–2	Kareem Abdul-Jabbar
1977–78	Washington Bullets	Seattle Supersonics	Washington, 4–3	Bill Walton
1978–79	Washington Bullets	Seattle Supersonics	Seattle, 4–1	Moses Malone
1979–80	Philadelphia 76ers	Los Angeles Lakers	Los Angeles, 4–2	Kareem Abdul-Jabbar
1980–81	Boston Celtics	Houston Rockets	Boston, 4–2	Julius Erving
1981–82	Philadelphia 76ers	Los Angeles Lakers	Los Angeles, 4–2	Moses Malone
1982–83	Philadelphia 76ers	Los Angeles Lakers	Philadelphia, 4–0	Moses Malone
1983–84	Boston Celtics	Los Angeles Lakers	Boston, 4–3	Larry Bird
1984–85	Philadelphia 76ers	Los Angeles Lakers	Los Angeles, 4–2	Larry Bird
1985–86	Boston Celtics	Houston Rockets	Boston, 4–2	Larry Bird
1986–87	Boston Celtics	Los Angeles Lakers	Los Angeles, 4–2	Magic Johnson
1987–88	Detroit Pistons	Los Angeles Lakers	Los Angeles, 4–3	Michael Jordan

1988–89	Detroit Pistons	Los Angeles Lakers	Detroit, 4–0	Magic Johnson
1989–90	Detroit Pistons	Portland Trailblazers	Detroit, 4–1	Magic Johnson
1990–91	Chicago Bulls	Los Angeles Lakers	Chicago, 4–1	Michael Jordan
1991–92	Chicago Bulls	Portland Trailblazers	Chicago, 4–2	Michael Jordan
1992–93	Chicago Bulls	Phoenix Suns	Chicago, 4–2	Charles Barkley
1993–94	New York Knicks	Houston Rockets	Houston, 4–3	Hakeem Olajuwan
1994–95	Orlando Magic	Houston Rockets	Houston, 4–0	David Robinson
1995–96	Chicago Bulls	Seattle Supersonics	Chicago, 4–2	Michael Jordan
1996–97	Chicago Bulls	Utah Jazz	Chicago, 4–2	Karl Malone
1997–98	Chicago Bulls	Utah Jazz	Chicago, 4–2	Michael Jordan

* The NBA had a Central Division in its first season, which was won by the Indianapolis Olympians, who were defeated in the second round of the playoffs

American Basketball Association

Season	Eastern Division	Western Division	Champion	Most Valuable Player
1967–68	Pittsburgh Pipers	New Orleans Buccaneers	Pittsburgh, 4–3	Connie Hawkins
1968–69	Indiana Pacers	Oakland Oaks	Oakland, 4–1	Mel Daniels
1969–70	Indiana Pacers	Los Angeles Stars	Indiana, 4–2	Spencer Haywood
1970–71	Kentucky Colonels	Utah Stars	Utah, 4–3	Mel Daniels
1971–72	New York Nets	Indiana Pacers	Indiana, 4–2	Artis Gilmore
1972–73	Kentucky Colonels	Indiana Pacers	Indiana, 4–3	Billy Cunningham
1973–74	New York Nets	Utah Stars	New York, 4–1	Julius Erving
1974–75	Kentucky Colonels	Indiana Pacers	Kentucky, 4–1	Julius Erving & George McGinnis
1975–76	New York Nets	Denver Nuggets	New York, 4–2	Julius Erving

APPENDIX G
Professional Basketball Statistical Records

(All statistics through 1997–98 season)

Career Points

Player	Seasons	Points	Player	Seasons	Points
Kareem Abdul-Jabbar	20	38,387	Karl Malone	13	27,782†
Wilt Chamberlain	14	31,419	Dan Issel	15	27,482*
Julius Erving	16	30,026*	Elvin Hayes	16	27,313
Moses Malone	21	29,580*	Oscar Robertson	14	26,710
Michael Jordan	13	29,277†	George Gervin	14	26,595*

* Includes ABA and NBA totals

†Active Player

Points Per Game/Season

Player	Team	Season	Avg.
Wilt Chamberlain	Philadelphia Warriors	1961–62	50.4
Wilt Chamberlain	San Francisco Warriors	1962–63	44.8
Wilt Chamberlain	Philadelphia Warriors	1960–61	38.4
Wilt Chamberlain	Philadelphia Warriors	1959–60	37.6
Michael Jordan	Chicago Bulls	1986–87	37.1
Wilt Chamberlain	San Francisco Warriors	1963–64	36.9
Rick Barry	San Francisco Warriors	1966–67	35.6
Michael Jordan	Chicago Bulls	1987–88	35.0
Kareem Abdul-Jabbar	Milwaukee Bucks	1971–72	34.8
Nate Archibald	Kansas City Omaha Kings	1972–73	34.0

Points Per Game/Career

Player	Seasons	Avg.
Michael Jordan	13	31.5†
Wilt Chamberlain	14	30.1
Elgin Baylor	14	27.4
Shaquille O'Neal	6	27.2†
Jerry West	14	27.0
Bob Pettit	11	26.4
Karl Malone	13	26.2†
Oscar Robertson	14	25.7
Dominique Wilkins	14	25.3
George Gervin	14	25.1*

* Includes ABA and NBA totals

†Active Player

Rebounds Per Game/Season

Player	Team	Season	Avg.
Wilt Chamberlain	Philadelphia Warriors	1960–61	27.2
Wilt Chamberlain	Philadelphia Warriors	1959–60	27.0
Wilt Chamberlain	Philadelphia Warriors	1961–62	25.7
Bill Russell	Boston Celtics	1963–64	24.7
Wilt Chamberlain	Philadelphia 76ers	1965–66	24.6
Wilt Chamberlain	San Francisco Warriors	1962–63	24.3
Wilt Chamberlain	Philadelphia 76ers	1966–67	24.2
Bill Russell	Boston Celtics	1964–65	24.1
Bill Russell	Boston Celtics	1959–60	24.0
Bill Russell	Boston Celtics	1960–61	23.9

Rebounds Per Game/Career

Player	Seasons	Avg.
Wilt Chamberlain	14	22.9
Bill Russell	13	22.5
Bob Pettit	11	16.2
Jerry Lucas	11	15.6
Nate Thurmond	14	15.0
Mel Daniels	9	14.9*
Wes Unseld	13	14.0
Walt Bellamy	14	13.7
Dave Cowens	11	13.6
Elgin Baylor	14	13.5

*Includes ABA and NBA totals

Assists Per Game/Season

Player	Team	Season	Avg.
John Stockton	Utah Jazz	1989–90	14.5
John Stockton	Utah Jazz	1990–91	14.2
Isiah Thomas	Detroit Pistons	1984–85	14.0
John Stockton	Utah Jazz	1987–88	13.8
John Stockton	Utah Jazz	1991–92	13.7
John Stockton	Utah Jazz	1988–89	13.6
Kevin Porter	Detroit Pistons	1978–79	13.4
Magic Johnson	Los Angeles Lakers	1983–84	13.1
Magic Johnson	Los Angeles Lakers	1988–89	12.8
Magic Johnson	Los Angeles Lakers	1985–86	12.6

Assists Per Game/Career

Player	Seasons	Avg.
John Stockton	14	11.3†
Magic Johnson	13	11.2
Oscar Robertson	14	9.5
Isiah Thomas	13	9.3
Kevin Johnson	11	9.2†
Mark Jackson	11	8.6†
Norm Nixon	10	8.3
Muggsy Bogues	11	8.2†
Rod Strickland	9	8.1†
Kevin Porter	10	8.1

†Active Player

APPENDIX H
Members of the Basketball Hall of Fame

Centers

Kareem Abdul-Jabbar
Walt Bellamy
Wilt Chamberlain
Dave Cowens
Neil Johnston
Bob Kurland
Bob Lanier
Clyde Lovellette
Jerry Lucas
Ed Macauley
George Mikan
Willis Reed
Bill Russell
Nate Thurmond
Wes Unseld
Bill Walton

Forwards

Paul Arizin
Rick Barry
Elgin Baylor
Bill Bradley
Billy Cunningham
Dave DeBusschere
Alex English
Julius Erving
Joe Fulks
Harry Gallatin
Cliff Hagan
Connie Hawkins
Elvin Hayes
Tom Heinsohn
Bob Houbregs
Bailey Howell
Dan Issel
Vern Mikkelsen
Bob Pettit
Jim Pollard
Dolph Schayes
Jack Twyman
George Yardley

Guards

Nate Archibald
Dave Bing
Al Cervi
Bob Cousy
Bob Davies
Walt Frazier
George Gervin
Tom Gola
Gail Goodrich
Hal Greer
John Havlicek
Buddy Jeanette
K.C. Jones
Sam Jones
Pete Maravich
Slater Martin
Dick McGuire
Earl Monroe
Calvin Murphy
Andy Phillip
Frank Ramsey
Oscar Robertson
Bill Sharman
David Thompson
Bobby Wanzer
Jerry West
Lenny Wilkens

Early Players

Caveman Barlow
Johnny Beckman
Bennie Borgmann
Joe Brennan
Tarzan Cooper
Forrest De Bernardi
Dutch Dehnert
Paul Endacott
Bud Foster
Marty Friedman
Laddie Gale
Pop Gates
Ace Gruenig
Victor Hanson
Nat Holman
Chuck Hyatt
Skinny Johnson
Moose Krause
Joe Lapchick
Hank Luisetti
Branch McCracken
Bobby McDermott
Stretch Murphy
Pat Page
John Roosma
Honey Russell
Ernie Schmidt
John Schommer
Barney Sedran
Christian Steinmetz
Cat Thompson
Fuzzy Vandivier
Ed Wachter
John Wooden

Women

Carol Blazejowski
Joan Crawford
Denise Curry
Anne Donovan
Lusia Harris
Nancy Lieberman
Ann Meyers
Cheryl Miller
Nera White

Foreign Players

Sergei Belov
Kresimir Cosic
Juliana Semenova

Coaches

Andy Anderson
Red Auerbach
Sam Barry
Ernie Blood
Howard Cann
Doc Carlson
Lou Carnesecca
Ben Carnevale
Pete Carril
Everett Case
Denny Crum
Chuck Daly
Everett Dean
Antonio Miguel-Diaz
Ed Diddle
Bruce Drake
Bighouse Gaines
Jack Gardner
Slats Gill
Aleksandr Gomelsky
Marv Harshman
Don Haskins
Ed Hickey
Howard Hobson
Red Holzman
Hank Iba
Doggie Julian
Frank Keaney
George Keogan
Bob Knight
John Kundla
Piggy Lambert
Harry Litwack

Ken Loeffler
Dutch Lonborg
Arad McCutchan
Al McGuire
Frank McGuire
Doc Meanwell
Ray Meyer
Ralph Miller
Jack Ramsay
Cesare Rubini
Adolph Rupp
Leonard Sachs
Everett Shelton
Dean Smith
Fred Taylor
Bertha Teague
Margaret Wade
Stanley Watts
John Wooden
Phil Woolpert

Contributors

Senda Abbott
Phog Allen
Clair Bee
Walter Brown
John Bunn
Bob Douglas
Al Duer
Clifford Fagan
Harry Fisher
Larry Fleisher
Eddie Gottlieb
Luther Gulick
Lester Harrison
Ferenc Hepp
Edward Hickox
Tony Hinkle
Ned Irish
William Jones
Walter Kennedy
Emil Liston
John McClendon
Bill Mokray
Ralph Morgan
Frank Morganweck
James Naismith
Pete Newell
John O'Brien
Larry O'Brien
Harold Olsen
Maurice Podoloff
H. V. Porter
William Reid
Elmer Ripley
Lynn St. John
Abe Saperstein
Arthur Schabinger
Amos Alonzo Stagg
Boris Stankovich
Ed Steitz
Chuck Taylor
Oswald Tower
Arthur Trester
Clifford Wells
Lou Wilke

Referees

James Enright
George Hepbron
George Hoyt
Matthew Kennedy
Lloyd Leith
Zigmund Mihalik
John Nucatola
Ernest Quigley
Dallas Shirley
Earl Strom
David Tobey
David Walsh

Teams

The First YMCA Team
The Original Celtics
The Buffalo Germans
The Harlem Renaissance

For More Information

Books

Gutman, Bill. *Shooting Stars: The Women of Pro Basketball.* New York: Random House, 1998.

Nabhan, Marty. *Men In the Middle.* Basketball Heroes Series. Vero Beach, FL: Rourke, 1992.

Sachare, David, ed. *The Official NBA Basketball Encyclopedia.* New York: Villard, 1994.

Telander, Rick. *Heaven Is a Playground.* New York: Simon & Schuster, 1991.

Wielgus, Chuck, and Alexander Wolff. *The In-Your-Face Basketball Book.* New York: Wynwood, 1980.

Wilker, Josh. *Julius Erving.* Black Americans of Achievement Series. Philadelphia: Chelsea House Publishers, 1995.

—. *The Harlem Globetrotters.* African-American Achievers Series. Philadelphia: Chelsea House Publishers, 1997.

—. *The Head Coaches.* Basketball Legends Series. Philadelphia: Chelsea House, 1998.

Wooden, John R., and Peter C. Bjarkman. Hoopla: *A Century of College Basketball.* Indianapolis: Masters Press, 1996.

For Advanced Readers

Axthelm, Pete. *The City Game: Basketball from the Garden to the Playground.* New York: Penguin, 1982.

Bayne, Bijan C. *Sky Kings: Black Pioneers of Professional Basketball.* Danbury, CT: Franklin Watts, 1997.

Pluto, Terry. *Loose Balls.* New York: Simon & Schuster, 1990.

—. *Tall Tales.* New York: Simon & Schuster, 1992.

Telander, Rick. *In the Year of the Bull: Zen, Air, and the Pursuit of Sacred and Profane Hoops.* New York: Simon & Schuster, 1996.

Internet

http://www.nba.com
The NBA's official site. Best are the biographies of the game's top players and coaches, written for the league's 50th anniversary celebration (go to www.nba.com/nbaat50/).

http://www.alleyoop.com
Up-to-the-minute news and statistics for both the pro and college games.

http://businesscents.com/cci/
A large trove of college-basketball history, including year-by-year summaries and features on the greatest teams and players.

http://httpsrv.ocs.drexel.edu/admin/vaughnmv/
The history of women's basketball, from its roots to the state of today's college, professional, and international competition.

http://cbs.sportsline.com/u/women/basketball
Excellent coverage of today's women's game, with features on NCAA action, the WNBA, and the ABL.

http://www.hoophall.com
The official site of the Basketball Hall of Fame in Springfield, Massachusetts.

http://www.remembertheaba.com
Photos, sound and video clips, and exhaustive lore from the heyday of the league that featured a red, white, and blue ball. A labor of love.

http://www.hoopsnation.com
A site devoted to the playground-basketball culture that continues to rear the stars we see on television. Lists all the top playground-basketball proving grounds across the nation.

Index

Page numbers in *italics* indicate illustrations.

About the Author

Mark Stewart ranks among the busiest sportswriters of the 1990s. He has produced hundreds of profiles on athletes past and present and authored more than 40 books, including biographies of Jeff Gordon, Monica Seles, Steve Young, Hakeem Olajuwon, and Cecil Fielder. A graduate of Duke University, he is currently president of Team Stewart, Inc., a sports information and resource company located in Monmouth County, New Jersey.